SERVING THE CITY

SERVING THE CITY

A celebration of sixty-five years of
THE BELFAST SOLICITORS' ASSOCIATION

Edited by Don Anderson

BLACKSTAFF PRESS

BELFAST

First published in 2008 by
Blackstaff Press
4c Heron Wharf, Sydenham Business Park
Belfast BT3 9LE
and the Belfast Solicitors' Association
Merrion Business Centre, 58 Howard Street
Belfast BT1 6PJ

Published in association with Ulster Bank

and The Law Society of Northern Ireland

Designed and typeset by IMD Typesetting and Design, Kent
Printed by W. & G. Baird, County Antrim

A CIP catalogue record of this book is available from the British Library

ISBN 978-0-85640-827-4

www.blackstaffpress.com
www.belfast-solicitors-association.org

CONTENTS

As chairman of the Belfast Solicitors' Association, I am delighted to introduce you to *Serving the City: A Celebration of Sixty-five Years of the Belfast Solicitors' Association.*

This publication charts aspects of the history of the Association from the war-torn 1940s, through the civil unrest of the 70s, 80s and 90s, and into the new millennium. It shows how the Association and profession have been at the forefront in adapting to the changing social, economic and, indeed, legal environment. However, this book is more than just a history – it is a snapshot of the profession as it currently stands and of its hopes for the future.

I am indebted to the past and present chairmen and members of the Association who have provided much valuable information for the book, and a special word of thanks must go to Joe Rice for initiating this fascinating project.

John Guerin
BSA Chairman

JULY 2008

I am delighted to have been invited to contribute to this publication which marks the sixty-fifth anniversary of the foundation of the Belfast Solicitors' Association. This is an important milestone in the Association's history. That it remains a vibrant and dynamic organisation owes much to the dedication and commitment of its officers throughout its life. Those who had the foresight and wisdom to establish this body and those who have served it so well over the years deserve great credit.

There is no doubt that the Association has brought Belfast solicitors closer together and has presented their views on all manner of issues in a coherent and effective fashion. It is not blinkered in its approach, however, and I know that it recognises the importance of its work and of its influence to the solicitors' profession generally, not just in Belfast but across Northern Ireland.

It is beyond question that challenges lie ahead for the legal profession in Northern Ireland, whether from the implementation of the review of legal services by Sir George Bain and his team or from the possible devolution of responsibility for justice to the Assembly. I am certain, however, that the Association will be ready to meet those challenges constructively and will do so in a manner that will bring conspicuous benefit to all the people of Northern Ireland.

I congratulate the Association on having reached this significant anniversary and wish it well for the future.

Brian Kerr

The Right Honourable Sir Brian Kerr
Lord Chief Justice of Northern Ireland

AUGUST 2008

Office of the
**First Minister and
Deputy First Minister**
www.ofmdfmni.gov.uk

Congratulations to the Association, and all its members, as it celebrates its sixty-fifth anniversary. There is much to celebrate and reflect on as over the years the Association has achieved much for all solicitors working here, not just for those based in Belfast.

For the people of the city, and beyond, Belfast solicitors continue to strive to deliver the highest possible standards of professional service to all. It is a level of service which their training, professionalism, traditions and their calling demand.

The dynamism and flexibility of the Association have allowed it to effectively meet many challenges over the past sixty-five years. There will no doubt be many more challenges over the coming years and with the breadth and depth of experience and expertise the Association, and its members, has it will address them in its typically energetic and enthusiastic manner.

Rt Hon. Peter D. Robinson
MP MLA
First Minister

Martin McGuinness
MP MLA
Deputy First Minister

AUGUST 2008

I am delighted to send greetings and good wishes to the Belfast Solicitors' Association on the occasion of the Association's sixty-fifth anniversary.

I congratulate the Association and its members on their contribution, on occasion made at some human cost, to upholding the rule of law through very difficult years, and on through the ultimate triumph of peace.

Mary McAleese

Mary McAleese
President

18 APRIL 2008

Reaching sixty-five years is a landmark age and the Belfast Solicitors' Association is to be congratulated on its continuous presence in the city since 1943.

Belfast has changed so much since the middle of the last century and the solicitors' profession, of necessity, has been at the heart of much of this transformation. It is difficult to think of any significant activity in the city, then and now, which does not require at some stage the input, expertise and skills of the solicitor.

We wish the Association well in its birthday celebration and anticipate it will continue to enhance the life of Belfast and its citizens for many years to come.

Councillor Tom Hartley
The Lord Mayor of Belfast

JULY 2008

✕✕ Ulster Bank

U lster Bank is proud to be associated with the Belfast Solicitors' Association. Now in its sixty-fifth year, the BSA has made a significant contribution to the legal process and business community within Belfast and Northern Ireland as a whole.

Belfast has experienced much change over the years. Today Belfast is an excellent city. World-class regeneration is taking place all around us, the city's retail offering is more dynamic and the business community continues to take risks and strive for bigger and better. The BSA and Law Society of Northern Ireland have contributed significantly to this change and most importantly will continue to do so in the future.

Henry Elvin
Head of Business Banking
Ulster Bank

AUGUST 2008

PREFACE

It has been my pleasure to work closely with solicitors for about a decade. I have dealt with public relations for the Law Society of Northern Ireland for roughly that period of time and I realised, while putting this book together, that I am irretrievably attached to the profession, and will hold it in high regard for the rest of my days.

I like solicitors. I like the calibre and personalities of the people attracted to the profession. Invariably, by the nature of their calling, they have a capacity to entertain difference, not a trait for which our society is widely noted, though we do seem of late to be getting a little better at it. Dealing in a civilised way with difference, whether it be across a court or across a desk, is the stock trade of solicitors. Even if they are conveyancing or dealing with probate, they are dealing with difference, with other parties – and with the divide between those who know procedure and those who do not.

I like lawyers because I like history. The history of the development of coherent society could be written as a history of the law and those who practise it. I like solicitors because, perforce, they must skilfully occupy an awkward niche. Solicitors are officers of the court; they hold an official position within the judicial structure, recognised universally as a profession, and yet they are also for the most part operating a business. If they don't sell their services, they don't have a living.

I like them because, as with accountants, medical practitioners and so forth, they have an entrée into parts of all our lives which are usually debarred to outsiders by a metaphorical notice reading 'Strictly Private. Keep Out'. Discretion is, of course, the middle name of each and every one of them. Solicitors can speak in general terms about the many messes that people get themselves into and out of, but not by way of specific illustration through the example of their clients. They may go about much of their business in public, but they remain professionally very private people.

The very judgement, discretion, tact, prudence and reserve with which solicitors must deal with a client's business do, I venture, put solicitors as a group at a disadvantage when required to trumpet their own occupation. I believe they find it difficult to switch roles to become strident advocates for their profession, much in the way it might be difficult for a librarian, living a life of hush, to become a leisure-time devotee of foghorns. Reticence and modesty prevail, perhaps to their collective detriment.

That is why a book like this is valuable. It unashamedly lauds what solicitors do. There are books about being a solicitor, but not much to read on the common experience of being a solicitor in a city like Belfast. A proper history of the profession in Northern Ireland is waiting to be written. In the meantime, these pages will give a few glimpses of the lives of solicitors and cast a little light on how a vibrant organisation like the Belfast Solicitors' Association came into being. It is a wide subject. Serious questions facing the profession are debated in these pages, but there is also revelation through anecdote of the fun to be had as a city solicitor.

Sixty-five years might at first glance appear an odd anniversary to celebrate. The Association celebrated its fiftieth anniversary and could have waited for the more usual seventy-five years anniversary before throwing another birthday party. But instinctively,

Association members may have felt that Northern Ireland's emergence from a generation of strife, which took its toll on the city, its people and its system of law, of which solicitors form an important constituent, was a line of demarcation worthy of acknowledgement. Time to look around afresh and take stock anew.

In putting this publication together I have had the unstinting assistance of the committee of the BSA under the able and energetic leadership of John Guerin. I am most grateful to John and to all the committee, whose names are listed in these pages. Many of the previous occupants of the chair have written articles or have agreed to the intrusion of protracted interview. My heartfelt thanks to them. The oldest of these earlier chairmen – and I know he will not mind that reference – is Victor Arnold, who was BSA chairman in 1968. By a pleasing accident of circumstance, that was the year John Guerin was born.

And, of course, there are the rest of the contributors who supplied further insight or delight or both. I am not a lawyer and there are many disciplines I am simply not competent to write about, certainly not for an informed and knowledgeable readership. The contributors gave freely of their time and expertise and I gratefully acknowledge that fact.

And there are those whose names will not otherwise appear in this book, but without whose help I would have faltered. I had goodwill and constant advice and help from the Law Society of Northern Ireland, its president, Donald Eakin (a past chairman of the BSA), chief executive, Alan Hunter, and librarian, Heather Semple. LSNI also granted permission for reproducing material from the book *It Was Like This Your Worship*, by the late solicitor and magistrate, Albert Walmsley.

The cartoons are by solicitor Rod Friers. Thank you, Rod. My gratitude also to solicitors Alan Hewitt and Donal McFerran, who provided much needed guidance. I am also indebted to Ken Murphy, Director General of the Law Society of Ireland, who directed me to *Portrait of a Profession* by Eamonn G. Hall and Daire Hogan, a history of the Society. I drew heavily upon this excellent and most readable work. Thanks also to Patricia Radcliffe, the librarian at the Bar Library, and to several members of the judiciary.

The small team at Blackstaff Press is talented. The cover design is by Lisa Dynan and the interior design and setting by Ian Mooney. I make special mention of editor Janice Smith, who has undergone a minor crash-course in law during the preparation of this book and whose attention to detail is meticulous – she would have made an excellent solicitor.

And I doff my cap especially in the direction of Joe Rice, past chairman and committee member. This book was his idea. Any failings and shortfalls in its execution are my doing, not his. He has been a constant source of both assistance and encouragement, allowing me to squat in his office and generally get under his feet. My thanks to him and to the staff of his company.

And my thanks to all of the BSA for drawing back the curtains on yet another window into a thoroughly interesting set of workers – the solicitors of Belfast.

Don Anderson

Introduction
DO AS LAWYERS DO

Joe Rice

Joe Rice is the senior partner of John J. Rice & Company (Belfast, Newtownards and Armagh), a deputy district judge and a board member of the Arts Council of Northern Ireland.

'Law and institutions are constantly tending to gravitate. Like clocks, they must be occasionally cleansed, and wound up, and set to true time.'

HENRY WARD BEECHER, *Life Thoughts*

'Reform! Reform! Aren't things bad enough already?'

attributed to MR JUSTICE ASTBURY, 1860–1939

The Belfast Solicitors' Association was established in 1943 as a voluntary organisation set up by solicitors in the greater Belfast area 'to ensure the provision of ethical and efficient legal services to the community' and 'to promote the welfare and interests of the legal profession in general'.

In recent years, changes to our society and to the law have been immense. Our move to a multicultural society is of such a scale that it could not have been foreseen even twenty years ago. The business environment, with globalisation and new regulatory frameworks and technology, has never experienced anything like the current pace of change. The challenge for our profession is to respond to these changing external pressures. We are still seen by too many people as a necessary evil, rather than providers of an added-value service.

The timing of this publication could hardly could be more auspicious, as we move beyond our sixty-fifth anniversary with an increasing membership. The number of solicitors practising in Northern Ireland has also increased: in 1943 there were 456 solicitors in independent practice here; in 2008 we have almost two thousand four hundred colleagues. And, indeed, one of the objects of the BSA as enshrined in the constitution is 'to publish, print, distribute and issue books, literature and information'.

It is often forgotten that Belfast was, for many years, the second city of the island, with status and importance to match. The solicitors of Belfast had an influence commensurate with the power of their commercial clients, but their role in the life of the city went far beyond that. There is hardly a school, a sporting organisation, a church or a social activity which did and does not benefit from the work of solicitors who donate leisure time to improve their own communities.

I was converted to the BSA cause around Easter 2002 by the then chairman, Stephen Andress. I met him, along with a young counsel, Frank O'Donoghue, at Vale do Lobo in Portugal. As well as being mightily impressed by Frank's golf swing, I was taken with Stephen's unbounded and infectious enthusiasm for the Association. He emphasised to me that the public is, as a rule, well served by our profession, but that there is no room for complacency. The Association was being proactive in promoting a series of radical modernising and consumer-empowering reforms, truly in the public interest, to ensure the right to the highest standards of independent legal representation and to protect the solicitor-client relationship. Over the years I have witnessed real changes in the direction and profile of the Association as it has adapted to an increasingly demanding business environment.

A new convert, as it were, I stood for committee a short time later at the AGM in the old Law Society House. From my first committee meetings under the

Law Society House is currently being built on the site of the Society's original three-storey office on Victoria Street

chairmanship of Peter Campbell, I was impressed by the cut and thrust of the proceedings held, religiously, on the first Monday evening of the month, with Frank McIlhatton, Richard Palmer, T.C. Smyth, Martin Mallon and others stirring up debate. So stirred up (and lengthy) did the monthly meetings become that by 2003 we had put in place subcommittees – Conveyancing, Litigation, Continued Professional Development and Social – which are now the engine-rooms of the Association, driving it forward.

Much of the early work involved preparing responses to a number of public consultations, including responses to various reviews of conveyancing, legal aid fees and litigation cost scales, and developing substantive interactions with government agencies such as the Court Service, the Legal Services Commission, and with our own, dedicated Law Society. The latter, through its hard-working secretariat and its presidents, offered continued access to its accumulated knowledge – Sue Bryson, John Bailie, Peter O'Brien and Alan Hunter merit special thanks.

I was conscious that our status as a representative body placed on us a responsibility to be vigilant to legislative and administrative development, bringing changes which not only affect the solicitors' profession but also the general public in Northern Ireland. We consolidated our position as a stakeholder to the consultative and analytical processes behind the making of our legislation.

Indeed, we maintained our position as the significant provider of Continuing Professional Development in legal education and enhanced our links with the Institute of Professional Legal Studies

through Anne Fenton, culminating in 2007 with the annual funding of three solicitor prizes at the Institute.

We re-forged our longstanding links with the Dublin Solicitors Bar Association, the Liverpool Law Society and the Mayo Solicitors' Association, to the mutual benefit of each association, and increased our contact with our local sister associations.

It soon became obvious that if the Association were to continue to go from strength to strength – and it was heartening during 2007 to see new corporate memberships coming from the public lawyers in the Public Prosecution Service and the Departmental Solicitor's Office thanks largely to Viv Harty's efforts – that we needed increased financing by way of sponsorship. Accordingly, we were fortunate to obtain significant sponsorship from First Trust Private Banking and we will always be grateful to David Allister and John Lilly of First Trust for maintaining their support.

The unselfish work of our Social Committee during my time with the Association has been dominated by three dynamic and enthusiastic solicitors, Sarah Havlin, Susan Brennan and Gavin Patterson. Their collective attention to detail is legendary, which makes our social events well-attended and memorable occasions. Sarah and Susan organise, on a regular basis, high-quality social events including nights at the races, quiz nights and the annual dress dance, which maintain the social profile of the Association. The additional sponsorship of BluePrint Appointments in relation to many of these events must be acknowledged. Having nominated the NSPCC as our chosen charity for the past three years, these events have proved to be an invaluable opportunity to collect funds for a most worthwhile cause.

We have moved a long way from committee meetings being held in the drawing rooms of office bearers, and we now have our own secretariat at 58 Howard Street, Belfast, where our administrator, Briege Williams – who manages to keep the ship afloat with no lack of good humour – is based.

Our website is continually developing and the energetic Keith Gamble deserves most of the credit for opening up cyberspace to the wider membership.

It has been an honour and privilege to be an office-bearer with the Association in the early years of the new century and I would like to pay tribute to the commitment of the many BSA committee members, particularly for the valuable time which they have given up to investigate issues for the benefit of the wider profession.

I can confirm that the talented and colourful characters of the legal profession that abound in the classic novels of Fielding, Austen, Trollope and, of course, Dickens, are still alive and thriving in the offices and courtrooms of Belfast. My own personal experience has been greatly enriched by meeting, through my contact with the Association, people of the calibre of Rosemary Copeland, Chris Ross, John Guerin, Viv Harty, Mark Shannon, Rod Friers, Niamh Lavery, Simon Crawford, Matt Higgins, Kathy Gordon, Toby McMurray, John Burke and Reg Rankin, to name but a few.

I know that the Association is well equipped to deal with our legal services environment, which will be in a state of flux in the short to medium term. The effect on solicitors and on their working environment is likely to be significant. Important issues and trends include new legislation influencing the nature and provision of legal services; the growth in the number of solicitor advocates; alternative dispute resolution; increasing demand for specialisation; a more robust competitive environment; and further financial restrictions.

The Association emphasises the importance of developing public awareness of the role of the solicitor. This will now include a more overt approach to promoting areas of work within each individual solicitor's practice. The Association intends to meet these new challenges and to that end will encourage its members to offer a personalised and efficient service which is accountable and of the highest quality. The solicitor is usually the first point of contact for any

member of the public seeking legal advice. Indeed, in the normal course of events, the solicitor is often the only point of contact, as he or she is qualified to see many matters through from beginning to end, for example in conveyancing, debt collection, making and dealing with wills, matrimonial cases and criminal advice in police stations and the lower courts.

The network of solicitors under the auspices of the Association, of varied experience, specialisations and seniority, helps to maintain and improve the standards of professionalism. Despite its conservative reputation, our profession and the BSA have been enthusiastically adapting to change for a long time. The quill pen has given way to the laptop. The Association will have a secure future as long as it continues to welcome reform of the legal profession that will make it more transparent and, thereby, increase public confidence. Chairmen and chairwomen may come and go, but it is the commitment of the wider membership that will ensure the Association's continuing success. One thing is for sure – where there are decisions to be made in private and public law, you will find colleagues from the BSA at the heart of the process, as we have been for the past sixty-five years and, hopefully, will be for the next.

Harcourt Street, Dublin, home of the Dublin Solicitors Bar Association

PAST CHAIRS OF THE BSA

First row, from left: Judge David McFarland; Henry A. Coll; Victor Arnold; Colin Gowdy; Donald Eakin;
Caroline Boston; Recorder of Belfast, Judge Thomas A. Burgess; Edwin Gibson

Second row, from left: Brian Stewart; Richard Palmer; Michael Davey; Raymond Segal; Niall Browne; John Guerin; Joe Rice

Third row, from left: Rowan White; Martin Mallon; Michael Leonard;
Neil Faris; Stephen Gowdy; Nigel Kerr; Steven Millar; Peter Campbell

Back row, from left: John Caldwell; David Flinn; Ciaran McAteer; Patrick White; Gavin Patterson;
Stephen Andress; Graham Keys

Missing from the photograph are George A. Palmer, Pauline Knight, Roger Watts, Frederick Haugh and Chris Ross

BSA TIMELINE

The BSA year of office runs from November to October. The years cited below indicate the start date of each chairmanship.

Date	Belfast Solicitors' Association chairs	Law and legislation events	Other events
1943	Robert Watts	BSA is formed: consitutional objects include maintenance of the highest professional standards; provision of a social programme; interaction with other local solicitor associations and with LSNI; and delivery of an efficient and effective service to the general public.	Basil Brook (Lord Brookborough) becomes third Northern Ireland Prime Minister. Eisenhower becomes the Supreme Allied Commander in Europe. Colossus computer developed to break German encryption. PGA Championship cancelled and Masters discontinued for the duration of the war.
1944	Robert Watts	BSA Constitution and Regulations formally approved by the council of LSNI. Ministries Act (NI), establishes a Ministry of Health with its own minister.	David Trimble born. Mount Vesuvius in Italy erupts and kills 26. Glenn Miller disappears while flying to Paris. Mairead Corrigan, Nobel Laureate, born.
1945	T.M. Heron	Northern Ireland Housing Trust set up under the Housing Act (NI). Criminal Justice Act (NI).	Second World War ends. First atomic bombs used against Japan. British take over Lebanon and Syria. Winston Churchill election defeat. 88 German rocket scientists taken to USA.
1946	T.M. Heron	Marriage and Matrimonial Causes Act (NI) extends the hours within which marriages may lawfully be solemnised.	Civil flights transferred to Nutts Corner from the Harbour Airport. Bikinis go on sale in Paris. George W. Bush, Stephen Rea and Camilla, Duchess of Cornwall, born. John Logie Baird, TV pioneer, dies.
1947	Albert J. Walmsley	Education Act (NI). Children to be assessed by tests at age 11 to determine what type of secondary school they will attend. (Only two non-grammar secondary schools in NI at this time.) Funding for Voluntary (Catholic) schools is raised to 65 per cent. Grants for third-level education open up universities to many less well-off people.	Coal nationalised. Partition of India and Pakistan. *Kon-Tiki* raft crosses Pacific. Golf (US Open) televised for first time.

Date	Belfast Solicitors' Association chairs	Law and legislation events	Other events
1948	Albert J. Walmsley	Health Services Act (NI) guarantees Exchequer funding for the first time to provide a health service equal to that in the rest of the UK. Belfast Corporation (General Powers) Act (NI). Transport Act (NI) set up the Ulster Transport Authority.	Gerry Adams born. Israel independence and the Arab–Israeli War. Berlin Blockade. Arthur Miller writes *Death of a Salesman*. Rory Gallagher born. Rugby drop-goal made 3 points instead of 4.
1949	Albert J. Walmsley	The Ireland Act gives first legal guarantee that Northern Ireland would not cease to be part of the UK without the consent of its citizens.	Maiden flight in England of the de Havilland Comet, world's first commercial jet airliner.
1950	George Leitch Snr	Children and Young Persons Act (NI) increases child protection.	Queen's University Belfast parliamentary seat at Westminster abolished. Ireland leaves the British Commonwealth and becomes a republic.
1951	Leslie Morris	Age of Marriage Act (NI) forbids marriage under the age of 16.	Festival of Britain exhibition in London. Oral contraceptive invented. Communist Chinese forces enter Tibet.
1952	D.P. Marrinan		Queen Elizabeth II succeeds George VI. European Coal and Steel Community, a forerunner to the EU, established.
1953	Robert McD. Coulter		Twenty-seven killed when a BEA Vickers Viscount strikes Nutts Corner landing lights. Korean War ends. Manchester University makes the first transistorised computer. First nuclear-tipped missiles deployed by USA. Tenzing and Hillary climb Everest.
1954	Robert McD. Coulter	Flags and Emblems (Display) Act (NI) gives the RUC a positive duty to remove any public flag considered likely to cause a breach of the peace.	US launches first nuclear-powered submarine and tests first hydrogen bomb. First Fender Stratocaster guitar. End of wartime food rationing in UK.
1955	Robert McD. Coulter		Television begins for Northern Ireland from the BBC transmitter on Divis Mountain. Xerox launch first office photocopier.

Date	Belfast Solicitors' Association chairs	Law and legislative events	Other events
1956	Robert McD. Coulter		Suez Canal Zone invaded by Britain and France.
1957	Robert McD. Coulter	School leaving age raised to 15.	Treaty of Rome sets up Common Market in Europe. *Sputnik*, first artificial satellite, launched by USSR.
1958	William J. Jefferson	Summary Jurisdiction and Criminal Justice Act (NI). Ulster Folk and Transport Museum set up by act of Parliament.	Belfast painter Paul Henry dies. Lagan canal from Belfast to Lough Neagh abandoned. Closure of numerous NI railway lines.
1959	William J. Jefferson		UTV launched.
1960	H. Harper Wilson		Death of inventor Harry Ferguson. Russian dogs successfully retrieved from orbit: the first living creatures to survive the experience.
1961	H. Harper Wilson	Rights of Light Act (NI) gives property owners a right not to have their light obstructed.	Stirling Moss drives Harry Ferguson's four-wheel drive P99 racing car to victory in the International Gold Cup at Oulton Park. Gary Player becomes the first foreign player to win the Masters.
1962	James O'Hara		Junctions 1–6 M1 open (but there are no junctions 4 and 5). Police run education programme to tell drivers how to use a motorway. First single issued by the Beatles. First commercial modem.
1963	James O'Hara	Caravans Act (NI). District Councils to keep a register of site licences.	Terence O'Neill becomes the fourth NI PM. Civil flights move from Nutts Corner to Aldergrove. President John F. Kennedy assassinated in Dallas.

Date	Belfast Solicitors' Association chairs	Law and legislative events	Other events
1964	T. Hall Dorman		Terence O'Neill is first NI PM to visit a Catholic school. First *Top of the Pops* broadcast with Beatles 'I Want to Hold Your Hand' at Number 1. Nelson Mandela sentenced to twenty-seven years in jail in South Africa.
1965	T. Hall Dorman	New Towns Act (NI) creates the framework for Craigavon.	Kings Hall Conference Centre built. Séan Lemass makes the first official visit by a Taoiseach to Northern Ireland.
1966	Thomasina McKinney	Last man hanged in Crumlin Road prison.	Queen Elizabeth Bridge over the River Lagan opens.
1967	Thomasina McKinney	Transport Act (NI) abolishes the Ulster Transport Authority and sets up a structure similar to that of today.	Last section of the M1 to Dungannon opens. BBC2 regularly broadcasts in colour. *Sea Quest*, one of the first oil rigs, launched in Belfast.
1968	Victor Arnold	Society of Labour Lawyers publish a report about alleged discrimination in NI. Electoral Law Act (NI) abolishes university representation and the business vote in Stormont elections.	New University of Ulster established. George Best nominated European Footballer of the Year and Football Writers' Association Player of the Year.
1969	Victor Arnold	Theft Act (NI). The Cameron commission established to consider the reasons for the unrest in Derry/Londonderry. Scarman inquiry into the causes of violence during the summer of 1969 in NI.	Ulster Troubles begin. First death of the Troubles. 'Temporary' peace line built in Belfast. First deployment of the army on NI streets. James Chichester Clark becomes fifth NI PM. New terminal at Aldergrove opens. Samuel Beckett wins Nobel Prize for literature. Man lands on the moon. *Sea Quest* makes first commercial oil find in the North Sea.
1970	Raymond Segal	Criminal Justice (Temporary Provisions) Act introduces mandatory 6 months prison for rioting. Estate Agents Act 1970.	SDLP and Alliance parties founded. Provisional Sinn Féin established.

Date	Belfast Solicitors' Association chairs	Law and legislative events	Other events
1971	Raymond Segal	Housing Executive (NI) Act becomes law. Decision to appoint a director of public prosecutions for NI announced. Internment introduced. Leasehold (Enlargement and Extension) Act (NI).	Brian Faulkner becomes sixth and last NI PM of the old Stormont parliament. First British soldier killed in NI. Ulster Polytechnic established at Jordanstown. DUP established. UDA formed.
1972	Frederick Haugh	Dublin Solicitors Bar Association presents BSA with chairman's badge of office. Welfare of Animals Act (NI). Widgery Tribunal, the first inquiry into Bloody Sunday. Scarman Report published into the causes of 1969 violence.	Direct rule after Stormont parliament prorogued. Bloody Sunday in Derry. Bloody Friday in Belfast. Temporary PIRA ceasefire and secret talks with British government. Mary Peters wins Olympic gold in the pentathlon. First pocket calculator. Troubles stop Wales and Scotland rugby teams travelling to Dublin.
1973	Frederick Haugh	Emergency Powers Act allows certain cases to be heard by a judge of the High Court or County Court, sitting alone with no jury (Diplock Courts).	First NI Assembly. UK, Ireland and Denmark join the EEC. Local government for the new 26 district councils. Proportional representation used in NI for the first time since 1920. Sunningdale Agreement on power sharing. The graphite golf-club shaft invented.
1974	Edwin Gibson	Internment ends. Westminster Prevention of Terrorism Act after Birmingham bombs gives powers to detain for up to seven days without charge and to allow authorities to 'exclude' people from entering Britain.	UWC strike brings down first power-sharing NI government. Dublin and Monaghan bombings by loyalists kill 33 people and an unborn child in 4 explosions. Approximately two hundred and fifty-eight are injured.
1975	George A. Palmer	Four get life imprisonment for 1973 Guildford pub bomb.	Temporary IRA ceasefire and more secret talks. John Luke, Belfast painter, dies. Ethernet developed to connect PCs together.
1976	Colin Gowdy	Solicitors (NI) Order to prevent solicitors acting when unqualified or bankrupt. Fair Employment (NI) Act gives effect to anti-discrimination provisions. Remission of sentences for NI prisoners raised to 50 per cent.	Betty Williams and Mairead Corrigan awarded Nobel Peace Prize. Temporary IRA ceasefire ends. First laser printer introduced by IBM.

Date	Belfast Solicitors' Association chairs	Law and legislative events	Other events
1977	G. Paul McRandal	Bennett Report into RUC interrogation methods set up.	First *Star Wars* film. Elvis Presley dies. Bing Crosby dies after completing a round of golf in Spain. Apple II computer with spreadsheet software Visicalc.
1978	Thomas A. Burgess		NI Westminster MPs increased from 12 to 17. First test tube baby. Space Invaders video game.
1979	Ruaidhri J. Higgins	Estate Agents Act. Eleven of the Shankill Butchers sentenced to total of forty-two life sentences	First European MPs elected from NI. Margaret Thatcher first UK female Prime Minister. Lord Mountbatten killed by IRA bomb. Pope visits Ireland. Compact disk invented. CompuServe becomes first service to offer electronic mail.
1980	Henry A. Coll	End of Special Category Status in NI prisons.	Microsoft commissioned to write the operating system for the PC. Indecency scandal at Kincora Boys' Home, Belfast: staff members charged with acts of gross indecency.
1981	Michael Davey	European Court rules against the British government for treating homosexuality as a crime in NI.	First section of the Westlink opens. DeLorean car first produced in Northern Ireland. IBM PC launched in USA. Bobby Sands dies on hunger strike. Northern Ireland's first religiously integrated secondary school, Lagan College, opens.
1982	Stephen Gowdy	IRA gun attack on LCJ Lord Lowry while visiting Queen's. Three of the five members of the Committee of Inquiry set up to investigate the Kincora scandal resign, claiming the police had not dealt with all the major criminal matters surrounding the case.	NI Assembly reinstated. Falklands War. DeLorean company, despite £80m in grants, closes with the loss of approximately one thousand five hundred jobs. British Enkalon in Antrim announces closure with loss of eight hundred and fifty jobs. Michelin at Mallusk announces closure with the loss of over two thousand jobs. Erica Rowe bares her chest during England vs Australia rugby match at Twickenham.

Date	Belfast Solicitors' Association chairs	Law and legislative events	Other events
1983	Niall Browne	County Court judge William Doyle shot dead by the IRA. In a supergrass trial in Belfast 14 UVF members are jailed for a total of 200 years. In another supergrass trial, 22 alleged IRA members are jailed for a total of over four thousand years. Thirty-eight IRA prisoners escape from the Maze. Edgar Graham, law lecturer and a UUP assembly member, shot dead by the IRA. Land Registration Rules (NI).	Belfast Harbour Airport (later Belfast City Airport) re-opens for civil flights. IBM PC European launch. Apple Lisa first computer with a graphical user interface involving a mouse, windows and pop-up menus.
1984	Pauline Knight	New Prevention of Terrorism Act allows the NI Secretary of State to proscribe certain organisations, to issue exclusion orders that prevent people from NI travelling to other parts of the UK or from travelling from the Republic to NI. Court of Appeal in Belfast quashes the convictions of the fourteen men who had been sentenced on the evidence of a UVF supergrass.	IRA Brighton bomb claims five lives and almost kills Margaret Thatcher. Miners' Strike UK. University of Ulster created out of New University of Ulster and Ulster Polytechnic. President Ronald Reagan pays a four-day visit to the Republic. Amstrad CPC 464 computer launched. John Stalker, deputy chief constable of the Greater Manchester Police, begins investigation into the alleged 'shoot-to-kill' policy of security forces.
1985	Nigel Kerr	The USA and UK sign a treaty that prevents the avoidance of extradition by claiming a political motive. Last of the supergrass trials.	*Titanic* wreck discovered. *Back to the Future* Hollywood film features the DeLorean car. Anglo-Irish Agreement signed.

Date	Belfast Solicitors' Association chairs	Law and legislative events	Other events
1986	Neil Faris	In an action brought by the Alliance Party, the High Court orders Belfast City Council to end the adjournment of council business in protest at the Anglo-Irish Agreement. The council has also to remove the large 'Belfast Says No' banner from the City Hall. New prison at Maghaberry receives its first prisoners.	John Stalker removed from the investigation into the alleged 'shoot-to-kill' policy of the security forces. Stalker was cleared of the allegations of misconduct and reinstated to his post but not to the inquiry. Chernobyl disaster. Smithfield Market rebuilt in Belfast. International Fund for Ireland established.
1987	David McFarland	Lord Justice Maurice Gibson of the Court of Appeal and his wife, Cecily, killed by an IRA bomb at Killeen. The judge is the fifth member of the NI judiciary to be killed by the IRA.	Enniskillen Remembrance Day Bombing kills 11, injures 63. First taxi driver to be killed in the Troubles shot by the UFF. Black Monday on New York Stock Exchange. First Rugby World Cup.
1988	Michael Leonard	Tom King, NI Secretary of State, announces legislation allowing a court to draw an inference from an accused person's decision to remain silent when questioned by the police. Remission of sentences for prisoners in NI reduced from 50 per cent to a third. European Court of Human Rights rules that by detaining suspects for more than four days, Britain was in breach of the European Convention of Human Rights. The UK decides nevertheless to retain a seven-day detention.	Stormont assembly dissolved. Hume–Adams meetings. Broadcasting ban on direct statements by those representing the IRA and other paramilitary organisations. Introduction of compulsory monitoring of the religious composition of workforces of all companies with twenty-five or more employees. Loyalist gunman Michael Stone kills three mourners at a funeral in Milltown Cemetery.
1989	Roger Watts	Police and Criminal Evidence (NI) Order. Prevention of Terrorism (Temporary Provisions) Act. New Prevention of Terrorism Act allows authorities to check bank accounts for paramilitary funds.	Fall of the Berlin Wall. Sky Television, first commercial satellite system in UK, launched. Home Office Minister, Douglas Hogg, is critical of a 'number of solicitors in Northern Ireland who are unduly sympathetic to the cause of the IRA'. Belfast solicitor Patrick Finucane, who had represented a number of Republicans, is shot dead by Loyalists the following month. Michael Stone jailed for 30 years.

Date	Belfast Solicitors' Association chairs	Law and legislative events	Other events
1990	Brian Stewart	Stevens Inquiry finds evidence of some collusion between members of the security forces and Loyalist paramilitaries. Room being used by the Stevens Inquiry destroyed by a fire. Broadcasting Act. Computer Misuse Act.	Taoiseach Charles Haughey makes official visit to NI. Castlecourt Shopping Centre opens. Nelson Mandela released from prison in South Africa. Brian Keenan released after being held hostage for 1,574 days in Beirut.
1991	Rowan White	Laganside Development (NI) Order provides for redevelopment of the city waterfront. Thomas A. Burgess becomes NI's first solicitor County Court judge. Birmingham Six freed on appeal after 16 years jail. Property Misdescriptions Act.	Berners-Lee's short summary of the World Wide Web project. USSR and Warsaw Pact military alliance dissolved. Robert Maxwell drowns. Fair Employment Commission announces that the display of religious or political symbols in work places might be considered intimidation.
1992	David Flinn	UDA proscribed. Judge Thomas Burgess leads the UK delegation to the Council of Bars and Law Societies of the European Community.	Teebane IRA bomb kills 8 workers in a minibus. IRA detonates huge bomb, estimated at two thousand pounds, at the forensic science laboratories in south Belfast, damaging seven hundred houses. Bill Clinton becomes US President. Intelligence gathering in GB moved from police to MI5. Irish People's Liberation Organisation disbands.
1993	Donald Eakin	Fiftieth anniversary of the BSA. Irish President Mary Robinson is guest speaker at the celebratory dinner. During a visit to west Belfast, Robinson shakes Gerry Adams's hand. The visit had not been approved by the government.	President Mary Robinson meets the Queen at Buckingham Palace, the first official contact between an Irish President and a British monarch. Ten die in IRA Shankill Road bomb. Hallowe'en Greysteel pub bombing kills seven in UFF revenge. Lagan Weir and M3 bridge completed. Belfast architect Dawson Stelfox climbs Everest.

Date	Belfast Solicitors' Association chairs	Law and legislation events	Other events
1994	Caroline Boston	Sir Louis Blom-Cooper, independent commissioner for the RUC holding stations, calls for video and audio recording of interrogations. LCJ Sir Brian Hutton judges the conviction of Paul Hill for the murder of a former British soldier in 1974 unsafe. Land Registration Rules (NI).	IRA mortar attacks on Downing Street and Heathrow. First IRA general ceasefire. Loyalist ceasefire announced. The Shannon–Erne Waterway reopens. Nelson Mandela becomes South African president. The British and Irish governments lift the broadcasting ban on Sinn Féin and other paramilitary organisations. Chinook carrying 25 security personnel crashes in fog in the Mull of Kintyre.
1995	Patrick White	For the first time, evidence is heard in a NI court relating to an attempted murder in the Republic. Criminal Appeal Act. Remission rate for NI paramilitary prisoners returned to 50 per cent. European Court of Justice rules that aspects of the Prevention of Terrorism Act contravene European Union law by impinging on the freedom of movement guaranteed by the Treaty of Rome.	Seamus Heaney awarded the Nobel Prize for literature. Bill Clinton visits NI, the first serving US President to do so. Commons Chamber at Stormont badly damaged by fire. Framework for Agreement published by the British and Irish governments. Prince Charles makes an official visit to Ireland – the first official royal visit since Irish independence. Trimble succeeds Molyneaux as UUP leader.
1996	Ciaran McAteer	Northern Ireland (Emergency Provisions) Act. Crumlin Road prison closes. Broadcasting Act.	Canary Wharf bombing ends IRA ceasefire. EU ban on British beef. Tiger Woods PGA Tour Rookie of the Year. Hotmail launched.
1997	Graham Keys	Criminal Cases Review Commission to review miscarriages of criminal justice in England, Wales and Northern Ireland.	Final IRA ceasefire. Tesco and Sainsbury's open first stores in NI. Waterfront Hall in Belfast opens. Divorce becomes legal in Republic of Ireland under certain circumstances.
1998	John Caldwell	Public Processions (NI) Act which outlines the powers and duties of the Parades Commission. Saville Inquiry into Bloody Sunday begins.	UFF and UDA ceasefires. Good Friday Agreement. Omagh bomb kills 29 people, the most deaths in a single incident since the beginning of the Troubles. NI Assembly elected. John Hume and David Trimble awarded Nobel Peace prizes.

Date	Belfast Solicitors' Association chairs	Law and legislation events	Other events
1999	Richard Palmer	Nuala O'Loan appointed Police Ombudsman.	Solicitor Rosemary Nelson killed by a bomb under her car. Full powers devolved to NI Assembly and power-sharing government. Launch of the Euro.
2000	Steven Millar	Terrorism Act. Michael Stone and other paramilitary prisoners released under the terms of the Good Friday Agreement.	Odyssey Arena opens. Playstation 2 launched. Joey Dunlop, motorcycle ace, killed while racing.
2001	Stephen Andress		Y2K computer bug fear proves groundless. 9/11 attacks bring down the twin towers of the World Trade Centre in New York. Apple iPod media player unveiled.
2002	Peter Campbell	Proceeds of Crime Act creates an Assets Recovery Agency, which made provision for confiscation in the UK, replacing separate drug trafficking and criminal justice legislation with a consolidated and updated set of provisions. It also sets out powers for use in criminal confiscation, civil recovery and money laundering investigations.	Power-sharing NI government collapses. Euro replaces the punt in the Republic.
2003	Martin Mallon	The Queen, accompanied by Prince Philip, officially opens the Laganside Courts complex. Access to Justice (NI) Order sets up the Legal Services Commission, which takes over legal aid and other services. New Bar Library completed in Belfast.	*Anvil Point*, last Harland & Wolff ship, leaves Belfast, ending one hundred and fifty years of shipbuilding. Iraq War.
2004	Gavin Patterson	Justice Act restructures courts with presiding judges appointed at each court tier accountable overall to the Lord Chief Justice. Saville inquiry final evidence.	Northern Bank robbery of £26.5m, one of the biggest bank robberies in British history. Madrid Train bombings kill over two hundred people. Belfast office block, Churchill House, demolished for new development.

Date	Belfast Solicitors' Association chairs	Law and legislation events	Other events
2005	Chris Ross		Underground bombings in London. George Best dies. NI beats England at Windsor Park. Hurricane Katrina floods New Orleans. Oil prices surge to record $60 a barrel.
2006	Joe Rice	Judge Burgess appointed Presiding Judge with responsibility for the County Courts. New era of 'Tesco law' in Legal Services Bill in the Queen's speech.	Belfast City Airport named after footballer George Best. Asda, the UK subsidiary of Wal-Mart, buys Safeway supermarkets. Last *Top of the Pops* TV show. Nintendo launches Wii games console.
2007	John Guerin	Northern Ireland Law Commission will be created under the Justice (NI) Act 2002, replacing existing non-statutory Law Reform Advisory Committee. The Commission will keep the law of NI under review, with a view to law reform. Al Hutchinson succeeds Nuala O'Loan as Police Ombudsman.	In May, NI Executive assumes control with the Rev. Ian Paisley as First Minister and Martin McGuinness as Deputy. Microsoft launches Vista OS. Ireland wins Triple Crown. Young Ulster golfer Rory McIlroy earns £186,645 in less than a month as a professional. O'Loan becomes a Dame in the New Year Honours on retirement.
2008		Belfast Solicitors' Association celebrates its 65th anniversary. Assets Recovery Agency merges with the UK-wide Serious Organised Crime Agency.	Victoria Square shopping centre opens in Belfast. Bertie Ahern resigns as Taoiseach and Brian Cowan takes over. Ian Paisley steps down as First Minister; Peter Robinson takes over.

Full weight of the law,
by Rowel Friers

Full weight of the Law

1 Judge F. Russell; 2 Judge J. McKee
3 Judge R. Babington; 4 Mr Justice Eoin Higgins; 5 Judge D. Lyttle
6 Judge J. Brown; 7 Judge R. Chambers; 8 John MacDermott LJ
9 Basil Kelly LJ; 10 Judge R. Porter; 11 Judge R. Rowland; 12 Judge B. Doyle
13 Judge Roy Watt; 14 Judge John Curran; 15 Turlough O'Donnell LJ
16 Maurice Gibson LJ; 17 Edward Jones LJ; 18 Robert Lowry LCJ

This cartoon is thought to have been drawn between 1979 and 1982.

REPRESENTATIONS OF THE PROFESSION

From the seventeenth century to modern times

Don Anderson

The establishment of the Belfast Solicitors' Association almost halfway through the twentieth century was not an isolated event. It was one of the later links in a chain of history spanning centuries and involving the cities of Belfast and Dublin.

Lawyers are authorised to provide legal services to the community, and admission to the legal profession has historically been regulated by the courts. For those readers who may not be lawyers, the courts have long recognised the right of a litigant to appoint another person as a representative in legal proceedings, and the two principal classes of lawyers – barristers and solicitors – evolved. Barristers are entitled to be heard in court and solicitors give instructions to barristers and act in legal proceedings during preparation for court hearings or in legal matters not involving litigation, such as probate and conveyancing. Solicitors were originally called attorneys, and the word survives in titles such as Attorney General and, of course – most clearly in the popular cognisance thanks to television and cinema – in the legal system of the United States.

During the late seventeenth and early eighteenth centuries, an informal method of admission to the legal profession in Ireland was modified by a number of statutes and by rules adopted by the Honourable Society of the King's Inns in Dublin. The King's Inns, founded in 1539, was an association of lawyers, governed by senior lawyers, including all judges who were known as the Benchers. In 1542, following Henry VIII's break with the Roman Catholic Church and the dissolution of the monasteries, the King's Inns was granted the land of a Dominican friary on the north bank of the River Liffey, a few hundred yards seaward of Dublin Castle. The King's Inns had considerable influence over both branches of the legal profession, barristers and solicitors.

An attempt at formal regulation came in the summer of 1607, when an order was made that the admittance of the practicers, officers, attorneys and others of the several courts whose 'auncientye' was not sufficiently known, be received and entered in a book 'as they shall appear and desire the same'. Thereby, solicitors and barristers in Ireland could become members of the King's Inns. Membership was voluntary. As in England, the solicitors in Ireland had no professional organisation, and although they were members of the Inn, they had no voice in the running of its affairs. Doubtless a state of affairs not to their liking.

In the late 1600s politics interfered in the regulation of the profession in Ireland to a point which would be undeniably illegal today. The cause was the *coup d'état* in England in 1688, when the dual monarchy of Protestant William of Orange and Queen Mary displaced Catholic James II, completing the process through a military campaign in largely

Catholic Ireland. In a Protestant state, fearful of counter-revolution and the restitution of a Catholic monarchy, Catholics were cast, if not as outright enemies in themselves, then as comforters of the enemy. Not the sort of people the ruling class wanted to have an important role in maintaining the law of a Protestant establishment in Catholic Ireland. For that reason, statutes were passed at the end of the seventeenth century and the start of the eighteenth century which tried to compel lawyers to take oaths and certain tests with the object of restricting the profession to members of the established church. The first of these statutes was passed in 1698. It baldly states that 'papist solicitors have been and still are the common disturbers of the peace and tranquillity of his Majesty's subjects in general'. Unless they came within the terms of the Treaty of Limerick (whereby defeated Jacobites, mostly Catholic, had their rights protected if they swore allegiance to William and Mary) which ended the Williamite war in Ireland, the legislation required solicitors to take oaths which were incompatible with the Catholic faith. The law does not seem to have been all that effective, since the situation required another more draconian law in 1707, with heavier fines because the existing ones were 'too small in respect of the great gains they make by their practice'.

James II died in exile in 1701, but it was not until 1766, when his son, who claimed throughout his life to be King James III, also died in exile, that the papacy recognised the 1688 constitutional settlement in England, and the pressure on Catholics began to lift.

In 1791, the beginnings of a grouping for solicitors started to take shape with the formation of the Law Club of Ireland in Dublin. Soon after, in 1793, the judges, possibly seeing in this club a loss of control over solicitors – and loss of revenue to the King's Inns – passed a number of resolutions affirming their control over the admission and regulation of solicitors and obliging all practising solicitors wishing to take apprentices to be members of the Inns. There was no law requiring solicitors to be members of the Inns, but as the Benchers were the judges of His Majesty's courts, they were in a position to lay down the conditions upon which practitioners could appear before them. The resolution began:

> We, the Benchers of the said Society, having full power and authority to make and ordain rules and orders for and concerning the business and practice of solicitors and for their admission into the said Society as members thereof [. . .] and being convinced of the importance of the trust committed to us, and that the safety and enjoyment of the persons, property, and character of the inhabitants of this Kingdom greatly depend on the knowledge and integrity of those who are permitted to profess and practice the science and business of the law, and conscious that as the grant of that permission is entrusted to us the reproach and crime will both be ours if at any time we shall admit into this Society any improper or incapable person, or, finding him grossly such suffer him to continue therein, and therefore that the means of information and improvement may be provided and held forth to all, and that the public may not be deceived by the sanction of this Society's name lavished upon the undeserving [...]

This must have added to the desire of the solicitors for professional independence. Despite constituting about half the membership of the Inns, solicitors were forbidden any governance of the Inns' affairs, and still had to pay the Inns' admission fees, annual subscriptions and, later, a proportion of the stamp duty on articles of apprenticeship.

However, in London in 1823, several prominent solicitors met to call for the formation of the London Law Institution, to raise the reputation of the profession by setting standards and ensuring good practice. The London Society was founded in 1825 and was granted its first Royal

There was no law requiring solicitors to be members of the Inns, but as the Benchers were the judges of His Majesty's courts, they were in a position to lay down the conditions upon which practitioners could appear before them.

Charter in 1831. A new Charter in 1845 defined the Society as an independent, private body servicing the affairs of the profession, like other professional, literary and scientific bodies. This set a new benchmark.

The Law Society of Ireland was founded in 1830 by solicitors. The annual subscription was £1 10s. 0d. (or £1.50 in modern currency) and its principal objects were the preservation of the rights and privileges of solicitors; the promotion of communication and good feeling within the profession; fair and honourable practice; to ensure respectability to the profession and advantage to the public; to oppose the apprenticeship or admission of unsuitable persons; and to erect a hall for the profession. A home was eventually provided by the Benchers in 1841 at the rear of the Four Courts in Dublin.

Solicitors in the northern part of the island could, of course, avail of the advantages of membership, but the northerners decided that they should have their own club and library, and established one in Belfast in 1843. Twenty-eight solicitors signed a prospectus declaring:

> We the undersigned Members of the profession of Attorney are desirous of establishing a Law Club with a Library in connection therewith in the Town of Belfast. We propose that the entrance fee shall be £3 3s. 0d. and the annual subscription £2 2s. 0d.

The library was housed within the Linen Hall Library in Belfast. The club aspiration was manifested later.

Two of the signatories to the prospectus were James Andrews, of 60 Donegall Street, Belfast, and James K. Jackson, of 6 Castle Lane, Belfast. In the Belfast *Street Directory* for the year 1842, the name of James K. Jackson is, with those of seventeen other practitioners, included under the professional description of 'Masters in Chancery', and he is recorded as practising in the Courts of Chancery, Queen's Bench, Common Pleas and Exchequer, and as being a commissioner for taking acknowledgements of deeds to be executed by married women.

The Law Society of Ireland was incorporated by Royal Charter in 1852. This was official acknowledgement of the Society's useful public functions and of the respectability of its members, but it still had no control over education and no say in the government of the Inns. The only law pertaining to legal training lay in provisions from the time of George II, by which an applicant was obliged to prove by affidavit that he had served an apprenticeship of five years. From the time of George III, moral examiners were appointed by the courts, but there was no proper test of legal knowledge. Perhaps it was at this time that the story of the examiner asking the candidate if he had been over the course originated. If not, he would then invite the candidate to set the text books on the floor and jump over them. 'Now,' the examiner would say, 'I can certify you have been over the course.'

Whether or not the story is true, there was enough truth in it to concern the Law Society in Dublin to push for reform. In 1860 the Benchers were persuaded to organise courses of lectures and to hold examinations to establish the fitness of those wanting to be apprentices and of apprentices seeking admission as solicitors.

The situation in Belfast at this stage is somewhat obscure. But in October 1861 a society was established for solicitors in Antrim, Armagh and Down. The following is from their rules and regulations:

I

That the Society now formed be called 'The Northern Law Club' and that it consist of the following original Members:

James Andrews, Robert Arthur, William E. Batwell, Samuel Black, Charles H. Brett, Samuel Bruce, James Campbell, Thomas Cary, William Carson, Alexander Caruth, Robert Cassidy, Robert Christie, James Cramsie, William C. Cunningham, Richard Davidson, John Dinne, John Ferguson, Joseph Gibson, Hugh Hyndman,

From the time of George III, moral examiners were appointed by the courts, but there was no proper test of legal knowledge.

Thomas B. Johnston, Robert Kelly, John B. Kennedy, Hugh Boyd Mackay, George F. McKeown, George L. Maclaine, Joshua M. Magee, Edmond Malone, Thomas McClelland, James McLean, William Orr, Alexander O'Rorke, Daniel O'Rorke, John Rea, Henry Seeds, William Seeds, Patrick Sheals, Robert W. Simpson, William Simpson, George K. Smith, Henry N. Smith, George Stephenson, Thomas Stott, Robert Ross Todd, James Torrens, George Gerald Tyrell, William T. Waterson, Esquires, and of such other Members of the Profession residing or practising in the Counties of Antrim, Armagh and Down, as may hereafter be admitted in accordance with the Rules and Regulations of the Society.

II

That the object of the Society shall be to watch proposed changes, either by Parliamentary enactment, or regulations of the Courts of Law or Equity, affecting practice privileges, and emoluments of the Profession of Attorney and Solicitor; and in connexion with other Societies; to oppose or promote them, as may be advantageous, by its intervention, when necessary, to sustain the rights and respectability of the Profession to prevent or adjust professional differences, and, by social intercourse to promote good feeling and harmonious action amongst its Members; and generally to undertake or assist in such objects as may appear to be conducive to the interests of the Profession or of the Society.

For solicitors, the enforced membership of the Inns was still most unsatisfactory and pressure from the profession resulted in the Attorneys and Solicitors (Ireland) Act, 1866, which was passed in the face of considerable resistance. Opposition included the Lord Chancellor of England operating on behalf of the Benchers of the King's Inns, because the Act removed the obligation for solicitors to be members of the King's Inns. Further, the legal education of solicitors' apprentices would henceforth be the responsibility of the Law Society, which would also now constitute the issuing authority for solicitors' annual certificates. However, the judges held on to the disciplinary jurisdiction.

Another important advance in the status of solicitors lay in the Supreme Court of Judicature (Ireland) Act, 1877, which provided that 'persons admitted as solicitors, attorneys, or proctors of or by law empowered to practice in any Court [. . .] shall be called Solicitors of the Court of Judicature' and:

> Any solicitors, attorneys or proctors to whom this section applies shall be deemed to be officers of the Court of Judicature; and that Court, and the High Court of Justice and the Court of Appeal respectively, or any Division or Judge thereof, may exercise the same jurisdiction in respect of such solicitors or attorneys, as any one of Her Majesty's superior courts of law or equity might previously to the passing of this Act have exercised in respect of any solicitor or attorney admitted to practice therein.

In 1878 the Northern Law Society in Belfast, along with the Southern Law Association in Cork, was given the right to nominate five extraordinary members of the council. To this day, the Law Society of

It Was Like This Your Worship — Albert Walmsley

The really good advocate has perhaps six or even ten points that are arguable, but what he will do is throw away the bad ones because generally speaking, there are really only one or at most two points that count in every case, and it is the duty of the man on the Bench to get down to the crucial point at the earliest possible moment. Many lawyers have the habit of exploring too many avenues of thought and only reach the salient point by process of elimination which can waste a great deal of time.

Northern Ireland sends members to a meeting in Dublin, usually once a year, but these extraordinary members by tradition refrain from voting and take no active part in proceedings. It has become a pleasant device for a meeting of the two societies.

The Act of Parliament that created the Law Society in its modern form and with functions recognisable today was the Solicitors Act (Ireland) 1898. It involved prolonged negotiations in which Edward Carson, barrister and ardent Ulster Unionist, cooperated closely with the solicitor and ardent nationalist, MP Maurice Healy.

This Act transferred the responsibility for legal education, examinations, and the appointment of lecturers and examiners from judges to solicitors, as represented by the Law Society of Ireland. Additionally, disciplinary functions passed from the Masters of Chancery to a statutory committee, and the custody of the Roll of Solicitors was transferred from the Court of Chancery to the Society – which, as it turned out, inadvertently nearly resulted in their destruction.

Not all solicitors were fully satisfied by the 1898 Act. The grumble in Belfast was that lectures were only to be given in Dublin and apprentices from northern parts had to travel down there to satisfy the requirements of the regulations. Aside from the politics of the time, this in itself would have caused negative feelings in Belfast.

The partition of Ireland has already been alluded to, but it merits more attention if only to highlight and make us appreciate what our solicitor forebears had to contend with. The break-up of political entities has almost become a

signature of our modern times. A similar series of political fractures happened after the First World War (and to a lesser extent, after the Second World War). Remarkably, in the time leading up to partition, two rival judicial systems were operating in Ireland, mostly in what is now the Republic.

After the end of the First World War in 1918, the conditions in Ireland became more unstable, with an increased number of lawyers sharing declining business. In 1920 Dáil Éireann set up its own courts and there was an associated policy of disruption of the established courts. Politics began intruding into ordinary legal business.

The Dáil Éireann courts had their origin in the national arbitration courts set up following a decree of Dáil Éireann passed in June 1919. These were generally local arbitration tribunals. One year later a full structure of parish courts, district courts, a circuit court and a supreme court was provided for by a new decree of the Dáil, and an alternative judicial system functioned openly in the summer and autumn of 1920 and again in 1921 after the truce in July.

In 1920 the IRA increased its disruption of the established judicial system, a task made easier by the War of Independence and civil unrest which was causing many offences to be tried in camera and in court martials instead of ordinary criminal courts. Magistrates were resigning, judges on assize were being refused accommodation and jury panels became reluctant to attend court. For example, in July 1920 the Westmeath County Council decided that all courthouses in the county would be closed and their government officials evicted.

The Irish Volunteers were asked to ensure that no judges entered the buildings for court hearings that were not recognised by the Dáil. Roscommon County Council decided to serve notice on the landlords of various courthouses throughout the county not owned by the council, stating that in future no rent would be paid as the courthouses were no longer required. That August, the Tyrone County Courthouse was burned.

Recollections   Victor Hamilton

The announcement in a Derry paper that the Lord Lieutenant had appointed Judge Walker Craig, then Recorder of Londonderry, to a judgeship elsewhere was followed by the words: 'The Lord gave and the Lord hath taken away. Blessed be the name of the Lord.'

The government retaliated by designating the Dáil courts as enemy courts. These enemy courts were to be boycotted. Public notices declared that anybody taking part in proceedings in an enemy court either as plaintiff, defendant, witness or whatever, unless with a special written permission of the Minister for Home Affairs, would be deemed guilty of assisting the enemy in a time of war and dealt with accordingly.

As partition loomed ever closer, the situation for a professional body seeking to represent solicitors across the board grew ever more shaky. Understandably, the Law Society of Ireland was trying to hold the profession together, taking the view that

> whatever division of Ireland for administrative and judicial purposes might be considered desirable, the status of the Society as the governing and educational body of the solicitors' profession in Ireland should not be affected, and there should be no division of the solicitors' profession, but all Irish solicitors should continue to have a right to practise in every part of Ireland.

With hindsight, this was a forlorn aspiration, but in the Society's defence it should be borne in mind that another profession, the chartered accountants, managed to maintain a single professional body, the Institute of Chartered Accountants in Ireland, which is still in existence today and exercising an all-island mandate.

With the publication in 1920 of the new Government of Ireland Act, which effectively partitioned Ireland, the Law Society in Dublin expressed the opinion that the establishment of separate judicial systems, north and south, was 'not a necessary consequence of the other proposals of the bill', and they supported an amendment unsuccessfully proposed at the committee stage of the bill to provide for the continuation of a single judiciary.

But matters were slipping out of the control of the Law Society in Dublin. In May 1920 the Northern Law Society decided to secure the same status and powers with respect to the north as the Law Society of Ireland had at that time for the whole of Ireland, dashing the hopes of the Dublin society of retaining its functions in relation to the profession throughout the whole of Ireland.

The Government of Ireland Act was enacted in December 1920, although its enactments for the South never happened. According to its provisions, from 1 October 1921 existing solicitors of the Supreme Court of Judicature in Ireland should automatically become solicitors of the Supreme Courts of both Northern Ireland and of the Republic, but thereafter (with an exception in the case of existing apprentices) new solicitors were to be entitled to practise only in the part of Ireland in which they had qualified. The profession was being split.

It is worth noting that in April 1922 the Four Courts buildings in Dublin were occupied by IRA members opposed to the Anglo-Irish Treaty, which had not resulted in the full Irish independence they felt they had fought for. In June, Irish government forces bombarded the building, which included the Law Society accommodation, causing very severe damage. Luckily, in 1899, a fireproof room had been constructed to house the Roll of Solicitors, custody of which had been granted to the Society the year before.

In February 1922 the Northern Law Society was granted a charter constituting it as the Incorporated Law Society of Northern Ireland, and in October the Parliament of Northern Ireland, sitting in Belfast City Hall because Stormont did not yet exist, passed a Solicitors' Act to give effect in Northern Ireland to the Solicitors (Ireland) Act, 1898, with certain modifications. The Incorporated Law Society of Northern Ireland continued to be represented on the council of the Law Society and initially, at least, northern apprentices continued to receive a part of their education in Dublin.

Relationships between the two societies were maintained. In 1926 the presidents of each dined in turn in Dublin and Belfast and the organisations cooperated in 1929

It is worth noting that in April 1922 the Four Courts buildings in Dublin were occupied by IRA members opposed to the Anglo-Irish Treaty, which had not resulted in the full independence they felt they had fought for.

to ensure that solicitors entitled to practise on each side of the border would not need to pay a separate licence fee in each jurisdiction. For solicitors in Northern Ireland the political upheavals were not so serious professionally because the fundamental structure of the court system and of the law was not immediately altered. But for solicitors in the South, it was all change. The Dáil 1924 Courts of Justice Act established for the Irish Free State a Supreme Court, a High Court, a Circuit Court and a District Court – a different structure to that of Northern Ireland.

The Northern Law Society Charter appointed Samuel Gordon Crymble the first president of the Society, John McKee and Samuel Ross the first vice-presidents, and provided

that Joseph Allen, Robert Baillie, Sir Charles H. Brett, John Dunville Coates, Joseph I. Donaghy, Thomas J. Elliot, Ivan B. Elliott, John M. Hamill, John B. McCutcheon, J. Charley McDowell, David West McGonigal, William McIldowie,

Charles A. McKenzie, Alexander S. Merrick, James Quail, James M. Pollin, Daniel Frederick Spiller, James C. Taylor, Martin Harper Turnbull, Robert Watts, George H. Wheeler, and James Wood shall be the Members of the first Council until the First General Meeting of the said Society for the Election of the Council shall be held.

On the day the charter was enrolled, the council met at Mayfair, an office building in Arthur Square, Belfast. Those present included David W. McGonigal, who acted as secretary. The minutes read:

The Charter of the Society was produced by the President and handed to the Secretary for safe-keeping. The members of the Council present expressed their sense of satisfaction that the Charter had at length been completed, and they heartily thanked the President for all the trouble he had taken in connection with the matter. As this was the first meeting of the Council

The Mayfair Buildings in Arthur Square

This portrait of James C. Taylor by the artist John Turner hangs in the offices of the Law Society of Northern Ireland.
It shows Taylor in the court dress he wore to the opening of the new Royal Courts of Justice in Belfast. The portrait was a gift to the Society from the Belfast Solicitors' Association, commissioned and paid for by the Association and presented on behalf of all of the membership. It was handed over by BSA chairman 1960–2, H. Harper Wilson, on the occasion of the Society's annual dinner in 1963.

LSNI & EWAN HARKNESS

of the new Society it was resolved that a new Minute Book be purchased. On the proposition of Mr. Robert Baillie, seconded by Mr. Samuel Ross the following Resolution was passed: That Mr. D.W. McGonigal be and he is hereby appointed Secretary and Treasurer of the Incorporated Law Society of Northern Ireland until a permanent appointment is made.

After payment of the fees on the charter, the Northern Law Society had a balance of

£75 12s. 3d. to credit in the Belfast Banking Company, Markets' Branch, Belfast. This account was closed and that sum handed over by Mr Ivan B. Elliott, the honorary treasurer, to the secretary and treasurer of the Incorporated Law Society of Northern Ireland.

The Solicitors Act (Northern Ireland), 1922, received Royal Assent on 26 October 1922, and Section 6 (2) provided that 'This Act shall be deemed to have come into operation on the tenth day of July, nineteen hundred and twenty-two', the date of the charter. Education regulations

With this minute in the records of the Law Society, the Belfast Solicitors' Association is tangibly linked with the centuries of manoeuvre, negotiation and, of course, politics.

were then established and lectures and examinations arranged by the Society.

On 11 February 1925, George H. Pollock was appointed secretary on the resignation of David McGonigal, and he established an office at 35 Royal Avenue, Belfast, where he practised in partnership with Mr Thomas Y.K. Mayrs of Pollock & Mayrs. The Northern Law Society's Library, now at Mayfair in Arthur Square, was used as the council chamber and lecture hall, and Mr Pollock's staff consisted of one clerk/typist.

The statutory duties of the Society continued to increase, but the money was insufficient. The Society had an annual grant of £200 from the Northern Ireland government, a good deal less than the annual £5,000 in stamp duties gathered by solicitors and payable to government. In 1932, with the approach of the opening of the new Royal Courts of Justice at Chichester Street, Belfast, its financial position was acute. Protracted negotiations took place, with the Ministry of Finance claiming a proportion of the stamp duties and for accommodation in the new Law Courts. The Society President, James C. Taylor, applied extreme pressure on the government right up to a face-to-face meeting with James Craig, who had succeeded Edward Carson as Unionist leader and was Northern Ireland's first prime minister. The Society did manage to locate suitable accommodation in the new Royal Courts of Justice, into which the office and library were moved in 1933. Though the accommodation had been sorted out, the financial dispute was not settled until January 1934, after the Society had threatened to surrender its charter and let the government make its own

arrangements for the governance of the profession.

The Second World War damaged Belfast severely. In April 1941, a night-time raid killed nearly a thousand people, destroyed half the city's housing, and left a quarter of the population homeless. However, two years later, despite the wartime austerity, food rationing and the wreckage surrounding them, a group of Belfast solicitors, in a gesture of optimism, inaugurated the Belfast Solicitors' Association.

Also in 1943, George Pollock was appointed Clerk of the Crown and Peace for the County of Antrim and City of Belfast. R. E. S. Johnstone took over the duties of Secretary of the Society and continued as such until the year 1946 when Lt. Col. R. Blair Mayne, DSO was appointed. Blair Mayne, a Second World War hero, Belfast solicitor and larger-than-life character, was killed in a car accident in Newtownards on 14 December, 1955. (The late Albert Walmsley, a noted Belfast solicitor and magistrate, wrote an appreciation of Blair Mayne and it is reproduced within these pages.)

In September 1944, the Council of the Incorporated Law Society of Northern Ireland included this paragraph in its minutes for 27 September: 'Resolved that the constitution and regulations of the Belfast Solicitors' Association as received from the Secretary of the Association be approved of without an amendment.' With this minute in the records of the Law Society, the Belfast Solicitors' Association is tangibly linked with the centuries of manoeuvre, negotiation and, of course, politics which constitute the history of the development of solicitors' profession on this island.

THE CALLENDER STREET MOB
The early days of the BSA

Edwin Gibson

Edwin Gibson, now retired, was a partner in T.M. Heron & Son, which merged with S.J. Diamond in 2001 to become Diamond Heron. He was chairman of the BSA from 1974–5 and was a member of the BSA committee for a quarter of a century.

To start at the beginning, I was born in Dundonald on the outskirts of Belfast. After Queen's I was apprenticed to the late Stanley Hill of Carson McDowell, qualifying in 1964. I began working as an assistant for Malcolm Davison in the firm of Hamill Davison.

Malcolm Davison was a great friend of Sir Lancelot (Lance) Curran, the High Court judge, later Lord Chief Justice, whose nineteen-year-old student daughter, Patricia, was found murdered in the grounds of her family home in Whiteabbey in 1952. The case was notorious at the time and became notorious again half a century later. A twenty-year-old RAF national serviceman, Iain Hay Gordon, was found guilty of the murder but declared insane. He was held in a psychiatric hospital in Antrim for seven years, released, and then spent the rest of his life fighting the verdict. (The culmination came in 2000 when his murder conviction was quashed by three judges of the Northern Ireland Appeal Court, marking the end of a long miscarriage of justice.)

I worked for Hamill Davison for about nine months, and then someone told me that I could earn more in the civil service than in private practice. So I joined the Ministry of Finance and after about two months I realised that it had been a mistake. I had to write legal opinions and found myself reading titles all day. Otherwise, I could only wonder at how one particular office colleague performed. He didn't open a file until 11 in the morning because he had first to finish his tea, smoke his pipe and then read the paper. Meanwhile most most of my departmental colleagues worked like Trojans.

One day in January or February 1966 I met a solicitor and fellow Instonian called Raymond (Ray) Segal in Corn Market and took the opportunity to ask if there were any openings he knew of. Ray was a partner in T.M. Heron & Son with Michael Heron. As luck would have it, a couple of days later he rang me up and said there was an opening as one of their two legal clerks was moving to another firm. The other clerk, Hugo Thomson, had joined T.M. Heron in or about 1909 and unbelievably was still working there in 1976. (It was said Hugo didn't read titles – he knew them all off by heart.)

I wasn't to know it then, but meeting Ray Segal that day in early 1966 was the beginning of a lifelong partnership and friendship. I joined the firm of T.M. Heron & Son, a move which soon connected me to

This picture was taken at the 1975 BSA dinner dance at the Culloden Hotel, outside Belfast. *From left* are Law Society secretary Sydney Lomas; his wife, Maureen; Rosemary Hamilton, who organised the event; 1966–8 BSA chair Thomasina McKinney; 1974–5 BSA chair Edwin Gibson; his wife, Carol; Detta Piggot; David Piggot from the Dublin Solicitors Bar Association; and the president of LSNI, Leslie Boyd.

EDWIN GIBSON

what became known as the 'Callender Street Mob', a group of solicitors who formed part of the committee of the Belfast Solicitors' Association. The firm of T.M. Heron shared a building with two other legal practices, Mills Selig & Baillie and John Johnson, now Johnson's. Next door were solicitors Peden & Reid.

Michael Heron, who was the senior partner in T.M. Heron in 1975, left and went back to England. For a while there was just Ray and myself. Then Graham Keys came in as an apprentice about 1978. He ultimately became a partner in the eighties, so there were three of us and the office became too small. I used to smoke the pipe and I had to give it up because while I was puffing you could hardly see out the window. So we moved round to Montgomery Street, taking over Osborne King & Megran's place. We remained there until 2001 when we merged with S.J. Diamond, becoming Diamond Heron. Ray retired in 1999.

Ray Segal was responsible for bringing me on to the committee of the BSA in 1968. With some reluctance I went along to my first committee meeting in the home of a colleague, Victor Arnold, who was chairman from 1968 to 1970. I was no sooner through Victor's door when someone said, 'You wouldn't like to take the minutes?'

On joining the committee I met the legendary Thomasina (Tommy) McKinney, an absolute pillar of the profession in Northern Ireland and a member of the BSA committee for many years. She also became the first female president of LSNI and indeed, the first lady to reach such a position in these islands. At all times, she was a great link between the BSA and LSNI, ensuring that if there ever was a risk of a clash, it would be of a minor nature at worst. Tommy was known and respected in legal circles throughout Ireland and across the water. Sadly, she died in 1988.

Shortly after I joined the BSA, I learned that there was an established practice of meeting with the Dublin Solicitors Bar Association. This was and still is an annual event, normally in the late winter or early spring. I think my first such meeting was about 1970, and I remember at that time wondering why most of our committee were going to the Ballymascanlon Hotel near Dundalk. There was never any sectarian or political edge to these get-togethers. The verbal and informal agenda was ostensibly to discuss matters of mutual interest, and I was puzzled as to what those might be. I quickly found that we were learning valuable insights into the Dubliners' approach to common problems and they, in turn, about ours. Such meetings ultimately had a major influence upon the BSA committee. But I also found the events to be great craic!

Many of the members of the Dublin Solicitors Bar Association appeared to have a much broader and more dynamic approach in dealing with problems facing their members, such as burdensome fee structures and procedures. The BSA appeared, by comparison, to be somewhat parochial. Often our members would write to the BSA committee for help with various individual professional problems and the Association would do what it could.

The Dublin colleagues held an annual dinner, which was a very grand affair, usually in the historic Four Courts on the banks of the Liffey. These were attended by two hundred or so solicitors and their guests, including some of the judiciary and the chairman of the BSA.

I remember that I was taken somewhat aback when I encountered the Dublin Taxing Master at the Dublin dinner, where he was well looked after, indeed sent home a happier man. Such contact with our Dublin colleagues caused some of our Belfast committee to think that we in Belfast were going about things in far too restricted a manner.

The other influence for change in our committee approach was our frustration with the then Law Society council, who at the time seemed to us like a pack of old duffers. Looking back, this view was probably extremely unfair, but nevertheless from our youthful vantage point, that was our perception. The LSNI approach seemed to us a bit pedantic, generating, in our frustration, a desire to explore other methods of dealing with matters and problems.

What our committee sought was general improvements, ranging from minor to major matters. For example, solicitors were then receiving what appeared to be a constant stream of practice directions from some of the Masters of the High Court and these directions carried a lot of force. You had to comply with them even if they appeared to be niggardly.

In the early seventies the great bête noire for us was the new Enforcements of Judgments Office. In the 1960s, a working party examined the administration and the adequacy of the existing methods of enforcing the judgments, orders and decrees of the Northern Ireland courts. As a consequence, radical changes were made to the systems for enforcement of all sorts of court orders, from recovery of debt to recovery of possession of house property. The system of under-sheriffs and bailiffs (in the South I believe they were known as 'grippers' – a great term) was replaced by a centralised unit in Belfast for enforcing judgments of the courts. So in 1971 was born the EJO, now under the umbrella of the Northern Ireland Court Service.

The new man in charge of the new EJO was the late Master Anderson. His practice directions were as numerous as fleas on a dog. It was unbelievable. Every week there was yet another lot of practice directions!

Shortly after the introduction of the system of enforcement, our committee formed the view that the easy bit was to obtain the enforcement order in favour of

More practice directions
ROD FRIERS

The volume of criminal damage and criminal injuries claims up until the 1970s had been relatively small, and now, suddenly, there were bombs going off every day.

our client. The hard part was trying to achieve enforcement of the order and that task was, in our view, being unnecessarily complicated by a stream of practice directions from the Master. Trying to resolve these enforcement procedures dominated the Association focus for quite a while.

It should be remembered that while we were acting primarily on behalf of our own members, when we did manage to achieve a measure of reform, it was often for the benefit of the whole profession throughout Northern Ireland.

Then there was the matter of achieving a satisfactory level of professional fees, a matter always close to our hearts. The fees issue divided into the contentious fees for work in litigation and the non-contentious, such as for work in conveyancing and probate. Initially we tackled the conveyancing fees. In the early seventies, conveyancing fees were governed by statute. The amounts were set out as two scales, a lower and higher. The lower scale covered about 90 per cent of the transactions. The statutory structure was not regarded as economic, but trying to change it was a nightmare. Eventually, we managed to have the statutory fee structure abolished in favour of an open-market fee scheme.

Once we got that out of the way, we set about dealing with the contentious fees structure – and it was the Troubles that brought some urgency to this problem. The volume of criminal damage and criminal injuries claims up until the 1970s had been relatively small, and now, suddenly, there were bombs going off every day. Under then existing systems, it was taking ages to sort out a 'bomb' claim and the fee structure was totally inadequate. The volume, complexity and size of cases did not match the fee structure. That was a real spur to move things ahead.

Next on our to-do list was the fee structure for personal injury compensation claims, mainly for road traffic accidents. We noted that the Dublin solicitors had a fee structure negotiated with the insurers and had created a fee guide. So we would try something similar. The result was a set of High Court fee

guides negotiated by the BSA with a committee representing various major insurance companies like Cornhill and Eagle Star Commercial Union.

Establishing these fee guides was a considerable achievement. The insurers eventually saw the advantages of a set fee structure, so when cases were concluded and compensation agreed, each side looked up the BSA guide and the fee was there. Previously, time was being spent by insurance staff bickering with solicitors about fees and occasionally pushing the issue into taxation. For solicitors a speedier closure meant that everyone got paid sooner. Insurers, too, saw advantage in speedier closure because it meant that they could adjust their figure flow accordingly. Every three or four years thereafter the fee figures would be revised.

We also had contact with the insurers to try to achieve a similar fee structure for County Court cases. The County Court already published a list of fees, so our negotiations with the insurers were related to the County Court cases settled by negotiation. It took a lot longer to negotiate an increase with the court service in the County Court fee scale, but it was facilitated when somebody eventually suggested asking the Recorder for Belfast, John Pringle, if he would have lunch with our committee – a step that initially put fear into some of our members. Many previous Recorders would not have been willing to meet our committee in such circumstances, but John Pringle was quite happy to come along and was very helpful in relation to certain matters of principle.

Having fee structures in place was not always a panacea. Up to the mid-1970s, when conveyancing fees were set by statute, at least there was the stability of knowing exactly what you could charge. Following the abolition of fees set by statute in the mid- to late 1970s, the resultant marketplace was a completely different circumstance. We found that some newly qualified solicitors cut the established scales of conveyancing fees. This understandably upset some members, but we could not have it all ways. It was now an open market, and that's what happens in open markets. Before, if you undercharged, it would have been a professional offence. However, the deregulation of conveyancing fees in my opinion was inevitable. If we had not taken the initiative ourselves, the politicians would have done it for us in time. In the end we had the comfort of the general acceptability of the BSA fee guides in both the contentious and non-contentious fields.

The next advance was to improve the social side of the Association for members. In the late sixties we had our first annual BSA dinner dance at the Culloden Hotel, a function which has gone from strength to strength ever since.

Then, about the mid-seventies, we started golf tournaments, first at Balmoral then at Malone. Some members were superb golfers. We, that's Ray and myself, were dangers to all those around us. One year at Balmoral Ray managed to hit not one parked bus, but two. After that, Balmoral was not all that keen to have us back, so we moved to Malone.

Moving back to setting our own house in order, we tackled the problem of differing holiday periods by circularising each year a set of holiday recommendations for Christmas, Easter, the Twelfth and so on. The aim was to achieve conformity. I remember a day or so after the Christmas holidays when Ray phoned a certain solicitor, a one-man practice, and was told he was away. Ray was then in a difficulty. He needed a cheque because his client was selling and buying. Thinking the man was merely out having a coffee, he inquired if he could speak to him later in the day. In a classic case of understatement, the secretary said there might be some difficulty because her boss was in Barbados, which resulted in much upset and shouting from Ray. This was precisely the kind of situation we hoped to prevent.

We also instituted annual committee dinners, to which wives and girlfriends were invited, to help bond the group

A working holiday?
ROD FRIERS

together. These evenings proved great fun, as well as being useful. Luckily, we all got on tremendously well, with no dissention. During my twenty-five years on the committee, I cannot recall any formal voting in committee – all decisions were based on the prevailing mood and the absence of dissent. For a bunch of solicitors this was little short of amazing. More seriously, the job of solicitor involves liasing with colleagues at practically every turn and this aspect of our everyday professional life helped to make the BSA committee function as a most harmonious body.

Someone on the committee suggested we should go away for a weekend together, again in the company of wives or girlfriends, where relevant. I think the committee weekends began in the late sixties and later lapsed, as these things can do, particularly since too often one person is landed with the responsibility of organising the events. I remember the late Tommy McKinney was always very good at organising such events. The destinations would be Carrygart, Bundoran and other places in Donegal. From these weekends

The badge of office of the chairman of the BSA, a gift from the Dublin Solicitors Bar Association

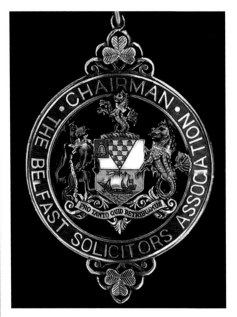

we began developing our links with other associations: with Dublin, of course, then with the Mayo Bar Association and the Liverpool Bar Association.

I have made mention of the influence of Dublin on our Association. They also influenced how we viewed ourselves and made us think about how others might see us. Our Dublin colleagues always looked the part. Their president, for example, appeared much more presidential because he had the trappings of a presidential figure, including a very nice badge of office, while all we sported were a couple of broken pencils!

In short, their presentation was always good and ours was a bit rough. In mitigation, with the onset of the Troubles, we perhaps had more things on our minds than presentation. Because of the conflict, we used to meet the Dublin Solicitors committee south of the border because no one from Dublin really wanted to come north. This suited us well and places like the Ballymascanlon Hotel were great for a one-night stay. Then in 1972, at one of the joint meetings, the Dublin Association presented us with a chairman's badge of office, which is magnificent. It set in train a process to achieve better presentation of the BSA. When I was in the chair in 1975, I ordered notepaper using our new badge as the basis of our logo. In other words, we have the Dublin solicitors to thank for shaping us up.

Having achieved a more visible, respectable posture in the late seventies, we felt increasingly confident in making contact with other professional associations and organisations which might be facing similar problems with, say, the Enforcement of Judgments Office. With that in mind, we began talking to the Association of Finance Houses because very often they were as frustrated as us in a shared context.

Both associations, the BSA and the Finance Houses, opened discussions with the Court Service about the problem with the Enforcement of Judgments Office. The Northern Ireland Court Service was set up in 1979 and its responsibilities included the operation of the troublesome EJO. We explained our difficulties to the Court Service, got tea and sympathy and little else. What next could we do?

We felt the answer was to lobby local politicians, which we had never done. With the help of the Rev. Ian Paisley we gained an audience with Peter Melchett (Lord Melchett), the direct rule minister at Stormont in charge of the Court Service. Unfortunately, we progressed little, but the exercise introduced us to the potential impact of lobbying members of parliament. After all, that was what they were there for, wasn't it?

Then along came the great Enoch Powell, a most effective MP who, frequently, at our committee's request, would raise questions in the house. He was very, very sharp.

We asked the Law Society to get involved in lobbying of MPs, but they appeared not to want to touch this tactic with a bargepole because, we felt, they did not think it was appropriate for the profession. This outlook has very much changed at the Law Society.

It was during the seventies that the Law Society secretary, Sydney Lomas, complained about a group of solicitors on the BSA committee, referring to them as the 'Callender Street mob', a nickname which stuck. The group included George Palmer of Peden & Reid, Ray Segal and myself. But by the mid-seventies, the whole committee of the BSA was seen as a ginger group, as might have been expected of young solicitors in their thirties and forties with a lot of spring in their heels. The Law Society council then appeared to us to be an older group, though again this is changing. Notwithstanding that our committee overlapped all over the place with the Law Society council, we usually succeeded in avoiding a clash, because that would not have done the profession much good. In the end the Society kept quiet and let us get on with it. So we succeeded but probably due to the good sense of Sydney Lomas, who was a quiet, sensible, effective man.

In the seventies the BSA did not have a full-time secretariat, and for the thirty years following it made things a little difficult at times. But this was offset by the enthusiasm of the committee. The committee meetings were always good natured, but we could have good scolding matches on occasion. In the mid- to late seventies, because of the Troubles, we were looked after very well. We met in the chairman's house, a pleasant practice (except perhaps for the chairman's spouse). It would occasionally be a sit-down meal for up to a dozen. Our wives were always very good about this.

We wanted to encourage the growth of other local solicitor associations. There always had been associations in Ballymena, Newtownards, Bangor, North Down, Enniskillen and so forth, but we understood they met mostly when the

occasion demanded. We began to request them to support us in various projects. If the BSA were to write to the Law Society with the backing of, say, half a dozen local associations, it would have all the more impact. Our success in encouraging other associations was limited, but the effort did raise interest in the governance of the whole profession and I believe manifested itself in more people becoming interested in joining the council of the Law Society.

The BSA adopted a subcommittee approach in dealing with various topics, such as changes in fees, legislation, practice directions and so on. These subcommittees would bring proposals to the main committee which, if passed, were put into action.

A major step was embarking upon educational lectures, an initiative that was very new in the late seventies and early eighties. We were probably the first to set up professional training lectures and the practice is now virtually an industry under the name of Continuing Professional Development – CPD. The aim, then as now, was to bring people up to date and to sharpen up practices.

The course of lectures started off in a small way with a couple of lectures in the year, and then it became four, usually held at the Law Faculty department of Queen's University Belfast in University Square at six in the evening. Professor Desmond Greer, then dean of the Faculty, was most cooperative and helpful. As the lectures became more popular, we moved them to Law Society House and started lunchtime lectures. From the outset we began producing a booklet of the content of each lecture.

There was no charge for lectures. We had to remember that joining the BSA was voluntary and if we had 50 per cent of the available Belfast solicitors, we were doing very well. We had to build up the association and the lectures helped with this. Today, I delight in the fact that the BSA is a strong, vibrant, professional organisation, hale and hearty, in its sixty-fifth year.

Edwin Gibson was talking to Don Anderson

By the mid-seventies, the whole committee of the BSA was seen as a ginger group, as might have been expected of young solicitors in their thirties and forties.

VICTOR ARNOLD
Life, practice and inspiration

Don Anderson

Victor Arnold began as an apprentice at Geo. L. Maclaine & Company, one of the oldest firms in the city. The founding father of the firm was James Andrews, who was admitted as an attorney in 1822 at the age of twenty-two and began his practice at 60 Donegall Street, Belfast. His father was the proprietor of a large flour mill in Comber.

George Maclaine, whose name is now above the door of the firm, was born in or about 1834. George's father, Alexander, was a partner in a Belfast shipbuilding firm, Ritchie & McLaine – the extra 'a' in Maclaine came later – which built the first steamship in Ireland. It is not known whether George was apprenticed to James Andrews, though this would seem likely, and he became a partner in 1858. 'Some,' Victor says, 'found him pompous and self-important!'

By the time of George's death the firm had its offices at 57 Upper Arthur Street, where they remained until 1922. The manner of his death is a salutary warning. The strongroom was out in the backyard, so not surprisingly there was a strict rule that it had to be kept locked at all times. One day in 1915 George, now about eighty, found it had been left open. His resultant great agitation brought about a fatal illness, and he died on 5 October 1915. Victor Arnold joined

Victor Arnold

the firm in 1950. He grew up mainly in the Cregagh area of Belfast. His father worked for the General Post Office in the city and was an ardent reader. Some of Mr Arnold senior's leisure time was spent browsing the second-hand bookshops in Belfast's old Victorian Smithfield Market, which was once a delight for hunters of serendipity. There was palpable sense of loss in the city when it burned down in 1974, to be replaced a dozen years later by a new Smithfield Market.

'My father bought instructional books to start with, and then progressed to second-hand copies of the masters,' Victor remembers. 'Sometimes he got out of his depth, such as when he bought Boswell's *Life of Johnson*, which is in two hefty volumes. He got through the first but got cast up on the shore with the second.'

(I reminded Victor that there was a good reference to lawyers in that book: 'You are a lawyer, Mr Edwards. Lawyers know life practically. A bookish man should always have them to converse with. They have what he wants.'

Victor replied that another reference was 'at last Johnson observed that "he did not care to speak ill of any man behind his back, but he believed the gentleman was an attorney." ')

The Arnold family home had exactly what the young Victor wanted, which was books galore. He acknowledges that this factor in itself gave him a fine start in life.

Around Easter in 1941 the family went on holiday to a rented house in the village of Portballintrae. While they were away, Belfast was bombed. Large parts of the city were devastated and more people lost their lives in the Belfast Blitz than in any single other air raid outside London: over 900 died and 1,500 were injured during the 6 hours of bombardment.

Victor's father decided that the family must remain in the village and he would commute from Belfast to Portballintrae at weekends. Some of Victor's childhood was then spent in and around Bushmills, where he went to school for a period, and to this day he has a great love of the countryside around that village.

Eventually, of course, the family returned to the city and Victor attended Inst: 'I went to Inst but hesitate to describe myself as an Instonian. You see, I'm not sporty and all Instonians have distinguished themselves to some measure in sport. Instead, I liked the countryside, walking in it and photographing it with a Brownie box camera.'

Like many others he learnt something of the excitement of natural history from the teacher, Dr Richard Burrows – Buggy to his pupils – who was sadly to lose his life on a European climbing holiday. His body was never found.

When he was about sixteen, Victor saw what he thought was a Vestal moth in the Castlereagh Hills and knew enough to realise that it was rare at that time in Northern Ireland. He took it to the museum, who referred it to Dublin, and he was told eventually that it was indeed a Vestal and only the third to have been discovered on the island. The finding was recorded in the *Irish Naturalists Journal* of 1946 in an article entitled 'Vestal Moth in County Down'. This simple discovery excited Victor more than any sport, but maybe it was a sport of a sort. (His account of the moth discovery can be now be retrieved on the internet!)

Victor attained what was known as a county scholarship to Queen's University. He very nearly started on a bad footing with the redoubtable Professor Montrose, dean of the Faculty of Law at Queen's. Victor was struggling to decide what course to follow at Queen's, whether it was

George Maclaine, whom the firm Geo. L. Maclaine & Company is named after

GEO. L. MACLAINE & COMPANY

James Andrews, the founding father of Geo. L. Maclaine & Company

GEO. L. MACLAINE & COMPANY

to be a BA in languages and classics, or in law. He thought he should talk to this professor, who was just a name to him at the time. With some hesitation he picked up the telephone, which he was still learning to use because it had just been installed in the house, and made an appointment.

Victor opened with, 'Professor Montrose, I would like you to advise me. I am thinking of doing a law degree – if I can – or an arts degree – if I can. At the moment I am leaning slightly in the direction of an arts degree because it would give me a wider cultural experience than a law degree.'

There followed a kind of explosion. 'I think if you were admitted to the law faculty,' replied Montrose, 'you would find our course is at least as cultured as the arts one – and in my opinion, much more so than the arts one.' But there was a twinkle in his eye and the two got on very well, notwithstanding this initial meeting.

The big names in the faculty were Professor Montrose and Professor Newark. The two men were like chalk and cheese. Victor remembers that Newark's lectures were typed out and from year to year the same lectures were given on each subject, sprinkled with occasional pieces of dry humour. He was a methodical and very good teacher.

Montrose was almost universally liked by the students because he was clearly a very idealistic man. Victor imagined he should have been a rabbi or something similar, and vividly remembers his first lecture from him in jurisprudence. The new law students all sat as eager as beavers, with notebooks in their hands and pencils sharpened. Then they heard this rotund man begin to speak: 'Ladies and gentlemen …'. This was the first item to raise their eyebrows. They had come straight from school, where they were called anything but ladies and gentlemen. 'I would like you to put away your writing materials,' the great man continued. 'I am not coming here to teach you to write. I want to teach you to think and I am not ever going to give you a lecture that you can take down like dictation.'

Victor Arnold inherited his father's love

of books, and to this day collects antiquarian volumes, often, though not exclusively, to do with the law. One of the volumes he encountered and found inspirational as a young man was by the eminent Belfast solicitor Charles Arthur Russell, Baron Russell of Killowen, GCMG, who was born in 1832 in Queen Street in the Ballybot area of Newry, and died in 1900. His father bought a brewery that provided a modest income. The family moved to Seafield House in Killowen, near Rostrevor, and then to Belfast in the 1930s. Russell began work in a local solicitor's office, Hamill and Denvir of Newry. Russell's boss, Cornelius Denvir, died in 1852, and the young man then left Newry to serve out his apprenticeship with Alexander O'Rorke in Donegall Street, Belfast. He completed his apprenticeship in January 1854 and soon established his own law practice in Donegall Street.

Before long, he decided to study for the Bar. He left his practice in Belfast to attend Trinity College Dublin, and then Lincoln's Inn in London. Within ten years he was one of the most highly regarded barristers in England and was appointed a Queen's Counsellor.

Russell served as Liberal MP for Dundalk in 1880, and later for Hackney in 1884. He became the first Catholic Attorney-General in 1886 under Gladstone. When Gladstone fell from power, Russell lost his position but he was reappointed in 1893. He went on to become Lord Chief Justice of England and Wales, the first Catholic to hold this post since the repudiation of Rome authority by Henry VIII. He was ennobled, taking the title of Lord Russell of Killowen, for the townland where he had grown up. His progression from south Down to the highest legal offices of an empire was remarkable.

Another mentor Victor chose for himself was Sir Edwin Herbert, who was a prominent name in the profession during the fifties. A distinguished English lawyer and president of the Law Society of England and Wales in 1956, he was also a celebrated mountaineer. So inspired by Sir Edwin and Lord Russell was the young

Victor Arnold that he copied their teachings out by hand, and he retains these notes to this day.

Most of Victor's work life was in the field of non-contentious, but, he observed wryly, it was surprising just how much non-contentious work was contentious. For example, he recalled the beginnings of the Troubles when the city was swamped with people who had been forced from their homes in droves: Catholics from Protestant areas, Protestants from Catholic areas. These people wanted to know what could be done for them. In the first instance, Victor saw, not very much. Belfast City Hall was submerged with claims for compensation but there was no effective machinery for providing such compensation.

'A claimant in dire need would send a notice of claim and get a response in about a month which asked him to furnish receipts for things like mattresses and chairs alleged to have been destroyed,' Victor recalls. 'This was being asked of unfortunates who had only what they were standing up in. A good man called David Creighton was the town solicitor in the City Hall at that time when this unprecedented situation landed on his desk. He had to set up a scheme of compensation, with its attendant documentation and he did his best. I think it all took its toll on him and he died of a heart attack.'

It was a mess that, of course, was sorted out eventually, but Victor and his colleagues all felt that work of this nature had to take precedence, and other more remunerative work must be set to one side. 'The nature of the profession,' says Victor, 'came to their aid.'

Law had always been a congenial profession and this played its part in extraordinary times like the early seventies. The pressures during the Troubles never broke up this fellowship and Victor knew that no one in the profession was ever going to operate against him on partisan grounds. It didn't matter a hoot who you were or who you were representing. All that mattered was getting the job done.

'It takes many skills to get a job done,'

Advice to a young solicitor

1 Begin each day's work with a menu of what is to be done in order of urgency.
2 Only do one thing at a time.
3 In any business interview, note in your diary, or in entries dictated to your shorthand clerk, the substance of what took place for corroboration in any future difficulty.
4 Arrange any case, whether for brief or for your own judgement, in the order of time.
5 Be scrupulously exact down to the smallest item, in money matters, etc, in your account of them.
6 Be careful to keep your papers in neat and orderly fashion. This you must be careful about, for I think you have a tendency to negligence.
7 There is no need to confess ignorance to a client, but never be above asking for advice from those competent to give it in any matter of doubt, and never affect to understand when you do not understand thoroughly.
8 Get to the bottom of any affair entrusted to you – even the simplest – and do each piece of work as if you were a tradesman turning out a sample of his manufacture by which he wishes to be judged.
9 Do not be content with being merely an expert master of form and detail, but strive to be a lawyer.
10 Always be straightforward and sincere.
11 Never fail in an engagement made, and observe rigid punctuality. Therefore be slow to promise unless that you can punctually fulfil.

Letter from Lord Russell to his son, Charles, 1888

says Victor. There is a story which the late Jack McCann, the prominent Ballymena solicitor, recorded for charity and which Victor loves to recount. It is very much about getting a job done. Jack was once instructed by a lady who owned a small dog. Unfortunately, the dog had nipped a child and the police wanted the little

So inspired by Sir Edwin and Lord Russell was the young Victor Arnold that he copied their teachings out by hand, and he retains these notes to this day.

animal destroyed on grounds of public safety. The lady sought Jack's help. In the resulting court case, Jack sat with the little dog beside him as he made his plea, relating the dog's good points. In the middle of his address, he broke off because the dog had begun licking his hand. At this, Jack asserted, 'Any dog that licks the hand of a Ballymena solicitor cannot be all bad.'

He won his case.

An address given by Sir Edwin Herbert, 1957

I would go so far as to say that the key to success or failure as a solicitor is your success or failure in giving to a client that sense of confidence that comes with the removal of his burden. If the burden has been removed they will be very ready to come and see you again – and to pay your bills upon which your living depends.

Absolutely the first condition in impressing a client is not to try to impress him. I have seen a great many reputations in the course of my life among solicitors go up like rockets and have seen them come down again like rocket sticks with the empty cartridge attached.

If a client comes into your office with a problem to be solved, much the best thing to do – indeed the only successful thing to do – is to solve the problem. And that means that you have got to make up your mind what the problem is. Behind every legal problem that is brought to you there is a human problem and it is upon that you should keep your eyes firmly fixed. Remember that all the technical problems are entirely subservient to that.

Would you please refrain from writing essays to your clients. That is no part of your task in solving their problem. You should make up your mind what you are going to advise your client to do. That is what he wants. Do not run off to counsel more than you can help. I would beg you not to be too much afraid of giving your own opinion, if you are quite clear in your mind what that opinion is.

Do not quarrel with the solicitor on the other side, even politely. While this ridiculous petty dispute is going on, the client's business is at a standstill. You will need particular forbearance and patience when the other side is demonstrably wrong.

A LIFETIME OF RESCUE AND RECOVERY

Sir Oliver Napier

Sir Oliver Napier, now retired, began his career in his father's firm in Belfast in the 1950s, specialising in insolvency and company rescue. He was a founder member of the New Ulster Movement, the first leader of the Alliance Party and a minister in the 1973 Northern Ireland Assembly.

My father was James J. Napier, who set up practice in 1929 just as the great recession was gaining ground. The major work then was insolvency and he quickly made himself an expert in that field, which I followed him into and so, in turn, did my daughter, Brigid. Specialising in that area was, looking back on it, a bit of a fluke because of the Wall Street Crash and its consequences.

My mother was a schoolteacher. My father was always going to put me into the business, though it would not have been my own first choice. I wanted to do agriculture, but my father told me there were only two jobs in agriculture: one was the Department of Agriculture, which didn't employ Catholics; and the other was employment in the Big House – a few of which still existed – and they wouldn't touch me with a bargepole. 'And,' he added, 'if you think I can afford to buy you a farm, you have another thing coming to you!' So it was to be the family business.

I was brought up partly in east Belfast and partly in the townland of Ballycruttle, outside Downpatrick, where I attended primary school. I went to Queen's in 1952 to do law under Professor Montrose. A wonderful man. He addressed freshers on their first day thus: 'Ladies and gentlemen, look to the person on your right-hand side, now to the person on your left. I want you to remember that two out of three of you will not be here next year.' In those days it was easier to get into law school than it is now, but they slashed the intake after the first year. If you did not get the exams at the end of the first year, you were out.

Also in those days students tended to be younger and less mature than the Queen's intake today, but that first year matured you speedily. It was brought home to you that the university, while it could be fun, was not a playground. University taught me how to think and I must give Montrose the credit for that because he was a great teacher.

He was fond of telling of two men looking out of prison bars. One saw mud, the other saw stars. He was relaying that if you clear your mind of inherited prejudices, you too can see the stars from what had been your prison. Montrose was a great influence in my life, even though for the first few weeks I was terrified of him. But very quickly I gained a tremendous respect for him.

I survived the exams. Nowadays there is a fashion for taking a year out, either before university or after. I would have loved to have done that, but if I had put

And so work begins
ROD FRIERS

the idea to my father that he pay for that, he would have gone ballistic. He could not wait, as a sole practitioner, to get me into the practice. As a family we were absorbed in the law. My younger brother Kit was also a solicitor, as was my sister Sarah. And four of my children are solicitors.

I continued to specialise in insolvency, and particularly in rescue schemes for businesses. Essentially my job boiled down to convincing the creditors of a company in trouble that if they did not foreclose, while they would not get all the money due to them, they would get some. My success rate was very near 100 per cent because I painted the horror story of what really happened in a bankruptcy. I made it clear that the only people to benefit in bankruptcy would be the liquidators and their legal team. 'They will love a bankruptcy,' I told them, 'and you, the creditors, will get nothing after the preferential creditors such as the Inland Revenue have been paid. The only way to stop that happening is if we all come to a deal.'

Many don't enter this field of the law because of the huge amount of work that has to be done before you can go to a meeting with the creditors. The first priority is to get the truth out of your client, which is not always the easiest of jobs. It is not so much a case of people telling lies; it is more a case of people in trouble overestimating their assets and underestimating their liabilities – merely because they cannot take the truth. So the preparation consists of getting from the creditors a true picture of the debt, and then painstakingly going through the assets of the debtor company and assessing accurately what they might be worth on the open market.

Only when armed with all this information can you proceed to put a deal on the table which has a chance of success. I could not afford to put up a deal which could fall apart. My reputation was that if Oliver Napier was putting up the deal, it would work. It was very important to me to guard that reputation: my father had been very good at this.

About 90 per cent of my work came from either solicitors or accountants. The

rest from bankers or by word of mouth. However, banks were not too keen on recommending me because they preferred to keep control of the client, getting his overdraft down and then throwing him to the dogs. Then new legislation came in 1991, the new Northern Ireland Insolvency Order, which followed the Insolvency Act 1986 in England. The order provided for people like myself to be licensed as an insolvency practitioner, meaning I could do all of the work myself and dispense with an accountant. My license number was 0001.

I worked very closely with the Inland Revenue and needed their trust. They would never have gone along with my rescue deals if they had not had complete faith in my figures. This had an important bearing in the case of the testimonial match in Belfast for George Best, who owed the Inland Revenue a lot of money. The testimonial match raised £72,000 and the Inland Revenue had heard of this. I was appointed by the liquidator in London as the Northern Ireland insolvency practitioner to see if the Inland Revenue could get the money. George had made promises of settlement of tax debts in the past to the Inland Revenue and their patience had run out. There was a very real danger that they would claim every penny of the testimonial match money. I realised that if all the testimonial money went to the government, it would be a public relations disaster. The testimonial match had been organised by decent, well-meaning trustees and football enthusiasts, and neither they nor the large body of fans in Northern Ireland who adored George Best would take kindly to such a move, to put it mildly.

The practitioner in charge of George's bankruptcy matters lived and worked in England. He phoned me and said, 'I think I would like senior counsel's opinion on this matter.'

I replied, 'Listen, I have senior counsel calling me up on almost a weekly basis to seek my advice, not the other way round. There are no senior counsel who know about this line of work. Why should we be paying a fee to any of them? This is Belfast, not London.'

I got the money frozen pending

This had an important bearing in the case of the testimonial match in Belfast for George Best, who owed the Inland Revenue a lot of money. The testimonial match raised £72,000 and the Inland Revenue had heard of this.

consideration. George was attempting to declare that the money was not for him, but was to be held in trust for his son, Callum. But that didn't seem to be convincing Inland Revenue. Nor was George in any position to get himself out of bankruptcy, which would have held the Inland Revenue at bay.

In the end I found myself in the driving seat. I said to the Inland Revenue, 'Like him or loathe him, George Best is a legend in Northern Ireland and if you take all the testimonial money, the effects on yourselves could be very serious. It would go down extremely badly throughout the whole community and could have repercussions. I have a suggestion. Let's split the money, half to Callum, half to yourselves. And you accept this as full and final payment, which will take George out of bankruptcy.' They agreed.

I was later disappointed never to have heard from George. He had been stating publicly that there was a 'knight' looking after his affairs in Northern Ireland and he was very grateful to him. But he never ever spoke to me. I think George Best thought that the world owed him a living. I would sum him up as a great footballer with a lot of personal problems.

There is still only a handful of insolvency practitioners in Northern Ireland. Naturally there is a close association with the work of accountancy and I consider myself to be a reasonably good accountant. I achieved a good knowledge of tax law and in fact I used to get quite a lot of tax investigation work sent to me by accountants whose clients were in trouble. The papers were sent to me with the idea of fashioning a deal because it was known that I had a good relationship, not only with Inland Revenue, but also with the likes of Customs and Excise.

Maintaining these relationships I considered very important, and sometimes it could be difficult, given that the personnel in these organisations are always on the move. However, nearly always I was dealing with people at the top, the chief executive and his second and third in command. People immediately below the top person

normally were in line to succeed when the chief executive either retired or moved on to another post. So there was some continuity.

However, the most important factor in this relationship was my reputation within Crown institutions as somebody who told them no lies. I made it my habit to put the case before them without frills or unnecessary embellishment. A plain honest assessment of my client's position. They knew that I had done my homework thoroughly and when I said, 'No, he doesn't have a house in Spain', they would accept my word. Once they were convinced of my integrity, then negotiations were fruitful for both sides.

The only person who ever came near wrong-footing me was Colin Lees from Magherafelt, a convicted drug dealer jailed for many years for conspiracy to supply drugs worth more than £31m. Lees plotted to bring amphetamines and ecstasy from Holland to the UK. The drugs, which were hidden inside pallets of jeans, were intercepted by police at a business unit in Rochdale.

In the late eighties and early nineties, Colin Lees was an entrepreneur held up as an example of great local enterprise by the Northern Ireland Office. Government minister Richard Needham was oblivious to Lees's dark side as he stood alongside him on the day the Magherafelt shopping centre Lees had built was opened. But behind the public front of the community businessman lurked an underworld. When his business finally collapsed, some £35m was owing. In addition there was fraud involving a missing £23m and a second crashed business in Scotland, owing nearly £20m. Lees also allegedly cheated a Texas businessman out of a million dollars and ruined the business of one of his father's oldest friends. That's before we get into the small matter of him laundering his own cash and that of the mafia, and running drug shipments into the British Isles. Quite a catalogue!

At one time I was representing Lees but I soon came to the conclusion that he was not being straight with me. I decided to dispense with him as a client because I simply did not trust him. There are two

The only person who ever came near wrong-footing me was Colin Lees from Magherafelt, a convicted drug dealer jailed for many years for conspiracy to supply drugs.

ways of getting rid of an unwanted client. One is simply to say that you are not going to work for him any more. The other is to say that you need £20,000 on account before you can proceed any further. From memory, I think I said to Colin, 'You already owe me quite a lot of money. I now need quite a lot on account', and that was the last I saw of him.

I was also involved in what was then the biggest bankruptcy case in Northern Ireland. The case was defended on legal aid – I did quite a lot of legal aid work – and there was a tremendous amount of work involved. The defendant went to jail for a long time and I submitted my fees in due course. It was a big bill reflecting the amount of work.

There was an interesting aside to that case, which was a criminal case. I fought it initially on the basis that under bankruptcy law you had to answer any question because it was a criminal offence to refuse. I argued that that provision could not be used in a criminal trial because if the bankruptcy rules were enforced, the defendant's confession had not been freely made. You are not required in a criminal case to incriminate yourself.

I lost. I then appealed on that basis and lost again. However, I am glad to say that I read a case in England about a year ago in which the proposition that I put up was accepted by the Court of Appeal. I was right. Otherwise all the prosecution has to do in a bankruptcy case that results in criminal proceedings is to read out the court notes and declare the defendant guilty by his own mouth.

I loved the intellectual jousting of the law. My father hated court and that was one reason he wanted me in the business as quickly as possible. Unusually, in insolvency cases a solicitor has right of audience in the High Court, and is entitled

to appear in insolvency matters and certain company matters. So I virtually never employed a barrister. My father also seldom employed one. But he loathed appearing in court because he had a very low voice.

He was a great friend of the late Lord Justice McVeigh. They were at Queen's together and wrote a book together entitled *The Law of Valuation*. McVeigh also had a very quiet voice. I was in court once with my father before I qualified. My father got up and said something I could not hear. Lord Justice McVeigh replied – and only the two of them knew what had passed, so quiet was the interchange. Nobody else heard anything!

In those days you qualified by doing three years' indentures, with an exam at the end of each year. From memory, my indenture was up on 1 July 1959. At that point you received your practising certificate at a ceremony. On a given day, everybody due to receive a certificate put on their best suits. They lined up in front of the Lord Chief Justice, who handed out the certificates. My father celebrated by taking a month's holiday! He said to me, 'Don't bother waiting for the ceremony. You go down today and get your certificate from the court office.' And this I did because I was due in court a day or two later.

And that was when I found myself alone on my feet in the High Court – indeed, in any court – for the first time, before Lord Chief Justice MacDermott. I got up and said, 'M'lord, I'm appearing in this case for the applicant.'

'I can't hear you,' said the Lord Chief Justice.

Now when I was at Queen's, I had taken part in many debates in the Literific Society and the Law Society. We debated with solicitors' apprentices from Dublin, Cork and Galway, and from England and Scotland. I had no trouble ever being heard – except on this occasion.

With greater projection, I said, 'M'lord, I'm appearing in this case for the applicant.'

'I can't hear you, Mr Napier!' the Lord Chief Justice repeated.

So I roared, 'M'lord, I'm appearing in

It Was Like This Your Worship   Albert Walmsley

The solicitor was trying to get some coherent account of events from his client, so at one point he asked the question, 'And then what happened?', to which he got the reply, 'Well he told me to go to the devil, so I came straight to you.'

this case for the applicant.' To which the Lord Chief Justice repeated once more that he could not hear me.

'Why?' I asked incredulously.

'Because you haven't got your practising certificate.'

I said, 'I have. Not with me, but it is in the office.'

I then told him how I had got it. He apologised to me. The problem arose because he knew that he had not handed me the certificate. I was auditor of the Solicitors' Apprentice Society – the equivalent of president. There was a tradition that if the auditor was a Catholic, he nominated somebody else to lay the wreath on Armistice Day. But I chose not to do that. I went myself to lay the wreath because I saw no reason why I should not honour the men and women who had died for us.

On that Armistice Day I had been ushered into a room awaiting the ceremony at the Royal Courts of Justice. The Lord Chief Justice was already there and asked if I was laying the wreath. I said I certainly was. We then had a long and interesting discussion. He had lost two brothers at the 1917 Battle of Passchendaele, also known as the Third Battle of Ypres. After three months of fierce fighting Passchendaele had been taken but at terrible cost. The Allied powers had sustained almost half a million casualties and the Germans just over a quarter of a

million in what turned out to be the last gasp of the 'one-more-push' philosophy. Its comparative failure and the horrendous conditions of deep mud in which it was fought made it emblematic of the dreadfulness of stalemated trench warfare. The Lord Chief Justice was therefore quite emotional about Armistice Day. As a result of that encounter he had remembered me and therefore knew that he himself had not presented me with a certificate.

But it meant that that day in court in July 1959, my very first on my feet, is burned in my memory for ever. I was nervous enough. Happily, nothing went wrong with the case and there was no subsequent ill-will on the part of the Lord Chief Justice. Quite the opposite. Upon occasion he would say to senior counsel, 'I can't hear you. Why don't you speak up like Mr Napier?'

I bought a holiday house in the late sixties, before the Troubles, near Kilcoo in the Mournes. It was a small house with about twenty-five acres of land on which I had cattle. The house wasn't big enough for all our children to sleep in so I bought a large caravan for the overflow. When the Troubles started certain people tried to petrol bomb the house. The damage to the house was not serious but the caravan was completely destroyed.

It was rumoured that this had been done by loyalists, but I did not believe that. I bought another caravan and fixed the house. One Sunday we left after a weekend to return to Belfast and, later that evening, the second caravan was burnt to the ground and the house very badly damaged. I knew by now it was the IRA making these attacks, and even got the names of the three people responsible. I got some local people to begin repairing the house in their spare time. They were working one night when the back door was kicked in and three men wearing masks appeared.

'Where's Oliver?' they shouted.

They told him I was not present and the masked men replied, 'We'll get him yet.'

They also put poison in the water trough for my cattle and three died. They would all have died if my neighbour had not seen what was happening and chased the cattle into another field.

After all that I knew I could not take my family or myself down there again. I instructed an estate agent to sell the place, but I stipulated that there were three people to whom I would not sell. Not to them, or anyone buying on their behalf.

'You can put that in the ad or spread it about any way you want. I will not accept any offer from those people,' was what I said to the agent.

Then I got a call from a man with the same family name as one of the people I would not sell to. He wanted to talk to me. He told me that the man I was against was indeed a relation, but that he genuinely wanted a house to live in because he was getting married. He gave me his word that he had nothing to do with the attacks and that he was not buying on behalf of his relation. He asked if I would accept his word on that, and I did. He bought the house and lived in it, which is what I wanted.

This was one of the aspects of life in Northern Ireland that made me become a politician. After what happened to me in Kilcoo I found that I could never be afraid again.

I managed to juggle my work as a solicitor and my political activity. I had a constituency secretary called Mavis Hogg, a lovely lady. I got up early in the morning and my first port of call was Mavis. I would give Mavis everything that had to be done that day. Then I went to my office. One

night a week I would have a constituency clinic, an advice centre in my home or my mother's home, which lasted for hours.

On Wednesdays I would go to see people who could not come to the advice centre, leaving the car in a fixed spot and walking round the streets, which is good politics. After eight or nine cups of tea and biscuits you might have felt like bursting, but you could not refuse.

At that time I had police protection, though it was nothing to do with what happened at Kilcoo. It was after an attempted assassination by the Official IRA, the Stickies, round about 1972. The perpetrators rang me up to go to a meeting in the Europa Hotel. There was ostensibly a delegation of young Conservatives who wanted to see me and I arranged to see them at two o'clock on Sunday.

But well before that time, a strong contingent of police came to see me and asked if I planned to go anywhere that day. I told them about the meeting and they told me not to go because it was a set-up. (I have no idea how they had discovered the plot.) They told me later that they had found a man with a machine gun in a phone kiosk opposite the Europa Hotel.

I then had police protection for quite a number of years. This stopped when the Rev. Bradford was murdered. He had had police protection at all times and was nevertheless shot dead. As chance would have it, the policeman escaped unhurt.

I then went to see the chief constable and said, 'What is the point of my having police protection in view of what happened with the Rev. Bradford?'

He said, 'Do you want a true answer?' and I nodded. He continued, 'The chances of them being able to save you if somebody wanted to shoot you are extraordinarily remote. Only if the gunman missed with the first shot would there be the slightest chance.'

'Then why are we wasting money on a police guard twenty-four hours on me?'

'You would have to authorise me to remove the protection – in writing. If anything happened to you the first question asked of me would be about the absence of police protection.'

So, in the late seventies, I signed the

> At that time I had police protection, though it was nothing to do with what happened at Kilcoo. It was after an attempted assassination by the Official IRA.

necessary papers and the police protection was removed. But while I did have the protection, I got an idea of how much work I was doing. The policeman was claiming ninety hours a week! He was probably right. Now I can hardly believe that. We had nine children and my wife would be walking to the shops with two in a pram and one who could hardly walk. There was no home help. And we thought nothing of it. My daughters and daughters-in-law would not even contemplate that. They would say it could not be done. But it was done, and by lots of parents all over the place then.

However, politics did obviously place an extra burden on myself and the family. And being involved in politics could be either an asset or a liability. I had clients come to me because of what I stood for and, conversely, clients who stayed away from my door for the same reason. My father was not in politics, but he did have clients who had nothing in common with him. He would not meet them in the golf club, or see them in his congregation. But if they had done something that they were somewhat ashamed of, this was exactly what they wanted in their lawyer.

There is little doubt that the middle classes and professional classes have for some time abandoned participation in politics, but I would advise young solicitors to become involved in politics. Politics have moved on dramatically. If anyone had said to me even a couple of years ago that Paisley would be First Minister with McGuinness his cordial Deputy, I would have said, 'You're dreaming.'

When I started in politics I did so within the Ulster Liberal Party under the Rev. Albert McIlroy. An eccentric but lovely man, Albert used to say that in Northern Ireland almost everybody said they were a liberal, and he believed them. And when the election came round, they took the ballot paper and just when they were about to put a cross next to the liberal, suddenly King Billy or Patrick Pearse appeared, as if in a dream, and the X went somewhere else. And the funny thing was that when they emerged from the booth, he concluded, they were convinced they had indeed voted liberal.

I started in politics to try to do two things. One was to counter the horrible sectarianism which I really only saw when I went to Queen's. The other was to galvanise the Catholic population. I thought that Catholics in Northern Ireland should stop accepting second-class citizenship. This existed only partly because it was imposed upon them, but also because they were accepting this. I felt that Catholics should play their part in Northern Ireland, that they should, for example, lay wreaths. They should work with the councils and Stormont. They didn't even have an official opposition in Stormont until 1969!

But the liberals had no party organisation on the ground and I thought this simply was not good enough. When this did not happen I joined others in setting up the New Ulster Movement, out of which grew the Alliance Party. The ethos was to have integration, respect and equality between Catholics and Protestants. We felt that you should not have to be a nationalist if you were Catholic and you did not have to be a Unionist if you were Protestant. That is why when we fought our first election in 1973, I stood in East Belfast and Bob (Sir Bob Cooper) stood in West Belfast.

So if I was addressing young solicitors now on the subject of playing a part in political life, I would make the point that things have changed greatly since the 1970s, that as a community we have come round to accepting each other's mandate. It means the party with the largest vote nominating the First Minister, and the second largest, the Deputy. We will survive by dealing with the issues that do not confront each of our fundamentals. We now have a structure which allows sectarianism to survive, even breed, but which also allows Northern Ireland to work. That's how I see it.

I would like to see a new wave of politicians who hopefully will take on the challenge of confronting sectarianism, which this system does not. Nevertheless, when all is said and done, what we have now is better than what has passed.

Sir Oliver was talking to Don Anderson

Politics have moved on dramatically. If anyone had said to me even a couple of years ago that Paisley would be First Minister with McGuinness his cordial Deputy, I would have said, 'You're dreaming, son.'

SHE WAS SITTING ON KING WILLIAM'S ACCOUNTS

Albert Walmsley

This is an extract from Albert Walmsley's *It Was Like This Your Worship*, published by the Law Society of Northern Ireland, 1988.

R.J. Adgey collected memorabilia to do with Northern Ireland. At the time I was making his will he gave me instructions about a valuable book, which was the original account-book of William III, Prince of Orange, during the period of his progress from Carrickfergus through Ireland.

It was a large well-bound, handwritten volume, kept by what nowadays would be known as the King's Treasurer. It revealed where the various monies in support of his army came from. The expedition to the Boyne took a number of months, and money was gathered in the various areas where he set up camp. A number of people were paid for giving information and other services. R.J. Adgey was very proud of this book and he wanted it to be displayed in Parliament Buildings along with many other treasures that the government of Northern Ireland had been presented with from time to time. Should they refuse to accept the book it was to go to Belfast City Council of which body he himself had been a member. After R.J. Adgey died I went to see Sir Norman Stronge who was Speaker of the House of Commons at the time.

He decided that if William III's account-book were put in Stormont it might cause controversy, and so he turned down the offer. It was of course a book of very great historical interest, and Belfast City Council were very keen to accept it. I am happy to say it is now on display in Belfast City Hall.

Actually getting it there was not such a simple matter. When I made the final arrangements for it to be received by the City Hall I went to find the book. It had been kept in a safe place in my office for several months until the negotiations were completed. Alas, to my horror the book could not be found, and days of searching did not reveal it.

Finally a young typist happened to say, 'I wonder would that book be the one that I'm sitting on?' and to my horror she got off her chair and produced the book, thank goodness none the worse for wear. When she had first seen the book she had decided it would be the very thing to put below her cushion, for she was small and the chairs in our office were too low for her. She never thought the book was valuable. The only thing I am thankful for is that she did not consign it to the bin.

Don Anderson adds:
In making sure that the City Hall still had the book, I contacted one-time Lord Mayor and long-time city councillor Sammy Wilson. He told me that he used to take parties of interested people round the City Hall and among the artefacts he would show was the accounts book. It was kept open at a page showing that the road from Newry to Dundalk had been paved on the orders of William so that his army could march faster south and on to the Boyne valley. The cost at the time was £16 3s. 2d. Sammy's commentary included the line, 'If they hadn't have coughed up that £16, maybe we wouldn't be in so much trouble . . .'

'I wonder would that book be the one that I'm sitting on?'
ROD FRIERS

THE BSA FIFTIETH ANNIVERSARY
An introduction

Don Anderson

When the BSA invited President Mary Robinson to its fiftieth anniversary dinner in June 1993, it brought about an event which has earned a place in the history of the evolution of the peace process in Northern Ireland. Notwithstanding the fact that the previous year Robinson had been the first President of Ireland to visit Belfast, this visit was very controversial, and led to John Major's government making its annoyance public.

The BSA had no idea that all this would happen when chairman Rowan White dispatched his letter of invitation back in June 1992, a full year before the dinner. For the BSA, the dinner was a celebration of an anniversary in the legal life of the city. The chief guest was recognised as one of the top legal brains in the UK and Ireland, a reputation earned well before she assumed the office of presidency. This was overwhelmingly the reason for the BSA invitation.

Context is everything. The road to peace was being constructed layer upon layer, but it was yet early days and there was no public perception of a process other than that of continued violence and political deadlock. Unionists were still smouldering in the aftermath of the Anglo-Irish Agreement, which the Garret FitzGerald coalition government signed with Margaret Thatcher's government in 1985.

The background to this particular visit was difficult. In March 1993, an IRA bomb in Warrington killed two small boys and outraged the public throughout the UK, Ireland and United States. The next month, another IRA bomb ripped through the heart of Canary Wharf, London's financial district, causing £350m worth of damage and killing a freelance *News of the World* photographer. A Great British public, long overtaken by tedium with regard to the Northern Ireland situation, became less sanguine and more resentful in the face of these attacks.

Mary Robinson attended the funerals of the Warrington bomb victims, and on 27 May visited the Queen at Buckingham Palace, the first meeting between the heads of state of the UK and the Republic of Ireland since 1937. Robinson was making her mark as a very different Irish President by repeatedly asserting her intention of addressing and acknowledging all the traditions on the island. She embarked upon this course from the outset by becoming the first Irish President to make the journey north of the border in an official capacity, and by visiting Northern Ireland four times within her first two years in office. Robinson had resigned from the Irish Labour Party in protest at the Anglo-Irish Agreement. She had argued that Unionist politicians in Northern Ireland should have been consulted.

In 2008 the Belfast Agreement is just ten years old, but already memories are beginning to fade as to what life was really like in Northern Ireland and Belfast during the Troubles. A list of violent acts carried out during this time could serve to jog memories, but a vivid illustration lies in the Law Society publication, *The Writ*, of March 1993. On a page devoted to the business of the BSA, there is a prominent announcement of the fiftieth anniversary gala dinner, with a slip to be cut out and sent with £25 to obtain a ticket (what good value!). But immediately below is a notice headed 'Terrorist Incident Rota'. It begins as follows:

> Following the massive bomb at the Forensic Science Laboratory and resulting damage to almost 1000

houses, the Law Society wishes to create a rota of solicitors who could attend an incident advice centre in the event of another incident. The Law Society has asked the Belfast Solicitors' Association to ask its members if they wish to be on such a rota [. . .]

That notice gives a flavour of 1993 and helps explain why the celebrations, which are recalled here by Rowan White and David Flinn, attracted so much media and political attention.

It Was Like This Your Worship

Albert Walmsley

One of my early cases involved a young man who was a defendant in a maintenance case at Belfast Magistrates' Court. He declared that he wasn't married at all because he could not remember getting married. His wife had taken proceedings against him because she said he had not supported her since the marriage had taken place. He said that the first time he heard about the wedding was the day after.

He remembered going to the house of the applicant – with whom he had been keeping company – and her mother gave him plenty of drink. He said it was the applicant's mother who suggested the marriage and the two women had filled him with so much strong drink that he did not know what he was doing. He had some hazy recollection of being in church, but he certainly never intended getting married. I cross-examined the wife about this, and she said that the marriage had taken place in church at nine o'clock that night. After the wedding she went home to her house.

This rather remarkable piece of pleading had no effect whatsoever on the presiding Resident Magistrate who said, 'Is their marriage certificate available? I see this marriage was witnessed by two people. I think the matter had better be adjourned for four weeks to allow one of the court officials – and perhaps even someone from the Registry of Births, Deaths and Marriages – to see if in fact a proper marriage took place.' Unfortunately these enquiries were of no use and my client had to pay the lady maintenance ever after. But then it is very difficult to get over a marriage certificate. The remark of the magistrate at the time was, 'If you were foolish enough to get married when you didn't have all your wits about you, then it's your own fault.'

The BSA in the
EIGHTIES AND NINETIES

Rowan White

Having practised
in Belfast and
Ballymena, Rowan
White was chairman
of the Antrim and
Ballymena Solicitors'
Association in 1983
and the BSA from
1991–2.

In September 1983, I returned to practice in Belfast, having spent the previous four and a half years in a firm in Ballymena. While in Ballymena, I had been a member of the Antrim and Ballymena Solicitors' Association and was chairman of it at the time I left to return to Belfast. I am probably unique in having been chairman of two separate solicitors' associations.

The ABSA used to meet on a fairly regular basis and all members were encouraged to attend and discuss whatever issues were uppermost in the minds of local practitioners at the time. Those practitioners were a fairly canny bunch and I suspect that some of them may have formed the view that holding office in ABSA was a chore that they could do without. Consequently, they had no compunction in putting keen but relatively junior and inexperienced colleagues (like me) in the frame. At the time I was elected chairman, I had only been qualified for five years!

On my return to Belfast, I was aware of the existence of the BSA and recall being slightly puzzled that it did not seem to provide a forum for its members to discuss matters of topical concern in the way that the ABSA had done. I eventually wrote to the BSA to query this and received a response from the then honorary secretary, David McFarland (now Judge McFarland), explaining the way the BSA operated. Because it was a much larger organisation than the ABSA, I was told it was not feasible for its members to attend every meeting and its day-to-day business was handled by a committee, which met on a regular basis. I was warmly invited to attend those

meetings and, when I took up the offer, was rapidly co-opted as a committee member. This was in late 1986 or early 1987.

Neil Faris was chairman at the time, and the monthly meetings were held at the offices of his firm, Cleaver Fulton Rankin. I only realised later that Neil was breaking with the tradition established in the 1970s of having meetings at the chairman's own house because of security concerns over attending evening meetings in Belfast city centre. One or two subsequent chairmen followed suit, but, for the most part, our committee meetings were held at the chairman's house and there was a lot of good-natured banter about the success of a chairman's year in office being judged, at least in part, by the quality of the suppers that he had been able to produce!

When I look back I realise that all of us put a very significant amount of time and effort into the BSA's activities. In addition to the monthly committee meetings, numerous ad hoc subcommittees were established to deal with specific issues, such as reviewing draft legislation, preparing for major social events or dealing with other issues which would have occupied too much time at monthly meetings. In addition, some members of the committee served as nominees on Law Society committees. For example, I served on the Home Charter and Education committees. Indeed, I still serve on the Education Committee, although no longer as a BSA nominee.

The committee meetings could be lengthy and occasionally slightly fractious, but were generally conducted in good spirit and with a fair degree of humour. I always felt that I got more out than I put in, as active involvement in the BSA was an excellent way to keep in touch with proposals and developments which would be likely to affect the profession at large in due course.

Having held the posts of honorary treasurer and honorary secretary in the preceding two years, I was elected chairman on 14 November 1991. The highlights of my year in office and, indeed, of the following year, arose to a large extent from the BSA's long-standing connection with the Dublin Solicitors Bar Association. It is probably fair to say that the level of contact between the two associations varied from year to year depending, largely, on the inclinations of the DSBA president and the BSA chairman. I was fortunate that the DSBA president in my year as chairman, David Walley, was particularly keen to promote contact between the two associations. Even before we had taken up our respective offices, he had floated the ideas of seeking a joint audience with the Irish President, Mary Robinson, and of BSA members participating in the DSBA's trip to Boston, Massachusetts, in the autumn of 1992. I am pleased to say that both ideas came to fruition. My fairly detailed recollections of those events, and of the fiftieth anniversary celebrations in 1993, are largely based on the diaries that I kept at the time.

An Audience with President Robinson, Saturday 28 March 1992

It is worth bearing in mind that the political climate in early 1992 was still fairly tense. President Robinson had made an official visit to Belfast, the first ever by a head of state of the Republic, on 4 February. The Law Society entertained her at a lunch to mark the 200th anniversary of the founding of the Law Club of Ireland (in which organisation both the Law Society of Ireland and the Law Society of Northern Ireland have their origins). I was a guest at that lunch in my capacity as chairman of the BSA.

Although President Robinson was widely regarded by Unionists as a friend of Northern Ireland, having resigned from the Labour Party in protest at the Anglo-Irish Agreement in 1985, the then Lord Mayor of Belfast, Nigel Dodds, snubbed her on her visit to Belfast on the basis that he could not greet the head of a foreign state which laid claim in its constitution to the territory of Northern Ireland. The *Belfast Telegraph* leader on 4 February pointed out that Northern Ireland did not have so many friends that it could afford to spurn them. However, thanks to the Law Society, while she may not have received a civic reception, she certainly received a civil one.

Even within a relatively enlightened organisation like the BSA, there was not complete unanimity over the proposed audience with the President. For example, DSBA's proposal that both associations should mark the occasion by making a joint contribution to Cooperation North was scotched after one committee member not only made the technical point that, under the BSA's constitution, charitable donations required the approval of the AGM, but also claimed that any publicity attached to the donation, even if made by individual members, would portray the BSA as the donor and that this would be improper because Cooperation North had 'political overtones'. In view of these sensitivities, I had the somewhat embarrassing task of explaining to David Walley that the BSA did not feel able to take up his proposal.

However, our visit to the President at Áras An Uachtaráin on 28 March was a memorable occasion, thoroughly enjoyed by the sixty or so solicitors present, including eighteen BSA members. On our drive out to Phoenix Park, David Walley and some of his colleagues had mentioned a rumour that that the President received a regular supply of free Guinness. It became apparent that this rumour just

President Robinson had made an official visit to Belfast, the first ever by a head of state of the Republic, on 4 February.

might be true when we were offered a glass of the black stuff along with, or instead of, a cup of tea! In her remarks to those present, the President highlighted the need to conduct cross-border relations in a less low-key manner, which she evidently felt our visit was an example of.

My year as chairman came to an end at the AGM on Thursday 12 November 1992, when I was succeeded by David Flinn. My diary records that in my report to the AGM I concentrated on the importance of communication to the existence of the Association. This was prompted to a large extent by the fact that I had gone to some lengths to re-establish contact with the Bar Council after a period of several years when there was little love lost between the two organisations. I had underlined the point by inviting the then chairman of the Bar Council, Patrick Coghlin QC (now Mr Justice Coghlin), and the chief executive of the Bar, Brendan Garland, to contribute to a discussion at the AGM on the need for change in the County Court system. They were both well received by an unusually large audience. At the risk of incurring the wrath of BSA members, I invited Pat Coghlin to chair the election of our officers, which he kindly agreed to do.

The BSA Fiftieth Anniversary, 1993

The preparations for the fiftieth anniversary began during my year as chairman. On 15 June 1992, I wrote to President Robinson and to the then Secretary of State for Northern Ireland, Sir Patrick Mayhew, to invite them both to attend a gala dinner on 18 June 1993. Both responded promptly to say that, official engagements permitting, they would be delighted to attend.

It was only after these invitations had been dispatched that I set about, along with other committee members, the serious business of raising sponsorship to defray the cost of the dinner. Northern Bank and Ulster Bank generously agreed to contribute £1,500 each and enjoyed joint-sponsor status as a result.

I recall having to work almost full time

on the preparations for the dinner in the week or so leading up to it. On Friday 11 June I received a request from both President Robinson and Sir Patrick Mayhew's respective offices for large quantities of information not only about the dinner itself, including the guest list (no doubt for security reasons), but also about the BSA. The Northern Ireland Office was particularly demanding, wanting the information that afternoon. In fact, they got it the following Monday as it took me a large part of the weekend to pull it together. The President's office then raised a number of points of protocol that had to be considered, and in some cases discussed with the Northern Ireland Office before they could be resolved. One issue was the order of speakers if the President spoke after dinner. This was resolved by having her speak before dinner. It was then suggested to us that, as a head of state, a toast should be drunk in her honour. This was a potentially sensitive issue but, after some deliberation, I suggested that we could deal with it by proposing a separate toast immediately after the Loyal Toast. Both the President's office and the Northern Ireland Office concurred and this is what happened. No one seemed in the least offended.

The day before the dinner, I was consulted as to what the President should wear. I was informed that she favoured a cocktail dress rather than a full-length one. I baulked at the idea of offering any advice on this delicate topic and immediately consulted Sue Bryson, the deputy secretary of the Law Society, who assured me that this was perfectly all right and that she too would be wearing a cocktail dress. I took the view that if it was all right for Sue, it should be all right for the President, who duly turned up attired in a striking midnight-blue cocktail dress!

We had arranged for a lady called Valerie McKee to bake and decorate a cake – a replica of Belfast City Hall. It turned out to be an absolute masterpiece, complete with dome. Transporting it to the Great Hall at Queen's University, where the dinner was held, was a potential nightmare, but my brother Patrick and I

Some colleagues had mentioned a rumour that the President received a regular supply of free Guinness. It became apparent that this rumour just might be true when we were offered a glass of the black stuff along with, or instead of, a cup of tea!

She encountered Gerry Adams on the Falls Road and allowed him to shake her hand. This was widely reported and provoked widespread controversy.

(he was also on the BSA committee and later became its chairman) managed this without incident. Our colleague, Jane Crilly, meanwhile, had been having difficulty persuading the authorities at Queen's to clear the Canada Room of stacked chairs. We had arranged to have a pre-dinner reception there and felt that the chairs were both an eyesore and taking up a lot of space. However, Queen's were adamant that they could not be removed. Jane ultimately persuaded them to do so, but only at the cost of disclosing the identity of our principal guest. This led to Queen's insisting on their vice-chancellor being present to greet her on arrival at the university, and to David Flinn inviting him to attend the dinner as an additional guest.

President Robinson arrived in Belfast in time to carry out other engagements before the dinner. In doing so, she encountered Gerry Adams on, I believe, the Falls Road, and allowed him to shake her hand. This was widely reported and provoked widespread controversy. I could be wrong, but I thought that I detected a distinct frostiness on Sir Patrick Mayhew's part when he greeted President Robinson at the dinner – no doubt due to the diplomatic incident which she had unwittingly precipitated.

Strangely, my recollections of the dinner itself are not as vivid as those of the events which preceded it. This may have been because I did not really feel able to relax and enjoy the evening until the dinner itself was over. I need not have worried; it passed off without mishap and was widely regarded as a great success.

Recollections
Colin Gowdy

Tom Hewitt was quite a character, as might be expected of an international rugby player. He was a solicitor who boasted that after qualifying some time before World War II, he never read any Act of Parliament or statute. He had a habit of speaking loudly down the phone. Admittedly the phones of the 1950s were not as efficient as those currently in use. The young solicitors (especially those who were acquainted with his sons and nephews) knew this. He would call and open with, 'Good morning.'

I would almost whisper back, 'Good morning Mr Hewitt.'

'Are you there?' he would shout even more loudly.

'Yes,' I would reply even lower.

'ARE YOU SURE YOU CAN HEAR ME?'

With a progression of hushed responses, the pantomime escalated until Tom was bellowing at the very top of his voice. It was said that Tom could have saved on phone bills by simply opening the window of his office and speaking with his telephone voice. I could not have seen him being happy with a mobile phone.

Recollections of the
BSA FIFTIETH ANNIVERSARY

David Flinn

David Flinn is a
consultant specialising
in the areas of energy,
renewable energy,
general commercial
law and employment.
He worked in-house
as a solicitor at
Northern Ireland
Electricity PLC and as
group solicitor of
Viridian Group PLC
over a period of
twenty-five years
years. He was chair of
the BSA in 1992–3
and is a former chair
of the Employment
Lawyers (NI) Group.

In 1992 there was debate among the Belfast Solicitors' Association committee about what to do to mark our fiftieth anniversary the following year. The idea of a dinner was mooted strongly. The main advocates were myself, Rowan White, Caroline Boston, Brian Stewart, Neil Faris and Donald Eakin. The more controversial discussions, however, centred around who to invite as the principal speaker.

Mary Robinson, the Irish President, was suggested. However, there were some on the committee who felt it was unlikely she would accept. Others believed that we were aiming too high. It was a brave suggestion at the time, as the Troubles were still in full flow and we knew the invitation would not be without political implications. It was unusual then, to say the least, to invite the President of Ireland to Northern Ireland.

Notwithstanding the political ramifications, there was a feeling that such an invitation was appropriate as the President was, after all, a respected academic lawyer. I think also there was a feeling that the invitation was a gesture appropriate to a more inclusive Northern Ireland. After debate, the die was cast, the President was to be invited and a dinner was to be held in the Great Hall at Queen's University.

A number of distinguished guests were invited. The first diplomatic incident was a phone call to the chair from Sir Gordon Beveridge, the vice-chancellor of Queen's. We had invited everyone to a dinner in the Great Hall at his university, but we had omitted to invite him! After some smoothing of ruffled feathers, the vice-chancellor agreed to come.

As I left home for the dinner at Queen's, affirmation of the importance of the occasion came with the news that the President had met Gerry Adams and shaken his hand earlier in the day on the Falls Road. At the time, this gesture on Northern Ireland soil was significant, as it was recognition of the leadership of Sinn Féin coming in from the cold. Prior to this, Sinn Féin was even banned from directly broadcasting in the media. It was, in effect, the beginnings of the peace process.

I must confess to being a tad nervous as I approached Queen's Lanyon building. The press were already there. Maggie Taggart of the BBC asked, could she film the President in the Great Hall. At first I said it was a private function, but then, under pressure, a compromise was reached whereby it was agreed that the media could film the beginning of the dinner and the arrival of the President in the hall. Caroline Boston, Donald Eakin and I greeted the President at the door of the Lanyon Building and then she and her husband, Nick Robinson, were brought upstairs for a small presentation prior to the meal. A Tyrone crystal gift was given to the President, to the Secretary of State, Sir Patrick Mayhew, and to the Lord Chief Justice, Sir Brian Hutton, to mark the occasion.

It was an honour to have two such distinguished lawyers present, Mary Robinson and Patrick Mayhew. Of course, the room was filled with judges and solicitors.

The President was introduced to Sir Patrick, Sir Brian, the vice-chancellor of Queen's, the president of the Law Society and other dignitaries. I was positioned between Mary Robinson and Sir Patrick at the centre of the top table with the Lord Chief Justice next to Sir Patrick. The thought did cross my mind that a well-positioned device could have disposed of us all very swiftly!

At the start of the dinner I proposed a toast to the Queen as head of state, and to the President of Ireland. This was again a diplomatic decision arrived at to ensure mutuality of respect. Then I made a welcoming speech, in which I announced it was an honour to have two such distinguished lawyers present, Mary Robinson and Patrick Mayhew. Of course, I realised the room was filled with judges and distinguished law society members and solicitors, so I said that, perhaps, I should mention this too. This went down with a laugh and was a good omen for the evening. Mary Robinson made a short speech of thanks.

The idea was then for the main course of the meal to be served and for Sir Patrick to make a speech at the end of this course. There was to be a short break before Sir Patrick's welcoming speech. In the break I was approached by the President's equerry, who informed me that the President was not well and would be unable to re-enter the hall for Sir Patrick's speech. I was somewhat shocked and said to the equerry that I was worried this might be perceived as a snub to the Secretary of State for Northern Ireland. Given the political climate at the time, the

implications of such a snub could be far reaching. Eventually, it was agreed the President would come in and stay for the speech.

I announced the President would be leaving immediately after the speech. At close quarters she looked pale and drawn. The day and the brave political gesture she had made had taken their toll (as, indeed, the equerry had told me). After the President left there was time still for an amusing speech from Tony Shiel, the president of the Dublin Solicitors Bar Association, and for convivial conversation. Sir Patrick asked a person at a table at right angles to the top table in what area of law he practised. To my consternation the recipient of the question seemed a bit bemused. It was only afterwards I realised he was a plain-clothes policeman. The top table was surrounded by them.

Once the dignitaries had left, there was time to relax and some of those on the committee retired to the Wellington Park Hotel. The evening had been a great success and had been headline news because of the political ramifications. It was, indeed, a gesture at the start of the peace process.

Sadly, the concept of mutuality of respect which the dinner symbolised would take some time to find expression of agreement between protagonists, and to be implemented in the political structures of Northern Ireland. It was another two years before the IRA ceasefire happened, a further five years until the Good Friday Agreement, and fourteen years before a power-sharing government was in place.

It Was Like This Your Worship

Albert Walmsley

Included in the [Resident Magistrate's] salary was a commuted forage allowance, though 'in order to be entitled to draw forage of £100 a year' he 'need not necessarily keep a horse'. One of my predecessors in Belfast was appointed in 1919 and drew this allowance until his retirement in the early sixties. He concluded – and he was probably right – that the forage allowance was really for the Resident Magistrate and was to be consumed in liquid form.

THOMAS A. BURGESS

The first solicitor judge in Northern Ireland

Don Anderson

I met Judge Thomas A. Burgess in his crisp, modern, even stark office on the top floor of the Laganside Courts complex. Somehow I had imagined that all offices inhabited by high judicial figures would be wood panelled, with parquet flooring entirely hidden by a deep-pile royal blue carpet.

But no. I was in a work space, a business office with none of the pomp and circumstance that might be expected as the trappings of the second citizen of the city of Belfast, which is the historical civic rank of the Recorder of Belfast.

So, although the occupant of this office had made history, there was little sense of history within the office. But there was from his office window, from which could be seen the lower portions of one of the old stone walls that may have been built along a carriageway leading to the River Lagan, in a Belfast long disappeared. This was uncovered when foundations were dug for a new building inside the Musgrave Street police station. Having been examined, mapped and documented by archaeologists, the walls have now been covered once more with ballast and concrete. Like the judicial system, cities are dynamic, layered new upon old.

Pride of place in Judge Burgess's office is given to the computer and workstation. In front of his desk is a table for meetings, which consume much of his time when he isn't sitting in court or working on judgments. He is proud of the information technology installed within the courts and demonstrated how quickly and easily he could locate and consult legislation and judgments on the computer system. He is also proud of the fact that Belfast is now regarded as a centre of excellence for IT in courts, and that Laganside has become a destination of pilgrimage for authorities in many parts of the world wanting to build new courts.

Judge Burgess made history when he was appointed Northern Ireland's first solicitor County Court judge in 1992. And he may have been the first judge to have been appointed without prior experience of criminal practice.

'My background had very little to do with the courts,' he explained. 'I had never been in a criminal court in my life until I appeared in a Diplock Court as a judge. I was born and bred a commercial lawyer and, therefore, the learning curve was particularly steep. The positive aspect of this, of course, was that there was no room for complacency and the discipline of thorough preparation was invaluable. To this day, I regard the trial and sentencing responsibilities of my work as among the most demanding, but also the most fascinating aspect of the job.'

Judge Burgess qualified in the mid-1960s and was apprenticed to his solicitor father, Alexander G. Burgess. In the early seventies, he joined Tughan & Company as a partner, heading their commercial and company law department – an area in which he was increasingly specialising. He

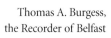

Thomas A. Burgess, the Recorder of Belfast

developed a formidable reputation for expertise, intellectual rigour and hard work.

Tom Burgess first involved himself in the broader aspects of the profession through the Belfast Solicitors' Association, becoming its chairman in 1978. He recalls:

'In our day we took the view that we could do everything the Law Society did, and we certainly could comment on everything the Law Society did. We did so, of course, with a total absence of the restraint of having to work within the constitution, and also of having to represent all the solicitors in Northern Ireland. Sydney Lomas, the then Law Society secretary, knew that within forty-eight hours of a BSA meeting he would have a list of the things which either the Law Society were not doing, or if they were doing them, were doing them totally wrong.

'The relationship between the two organisations was all the more interesting for that reason. The BSA was a true ginger group, always pressing the case for solicitors without the restraint which governed the Law Society – that of protecting a public interest – and it was not open to the Law Society to operate simply as a trade union.

'If you became a member of the Law Society council and you were a member of the BSA committee, it was expected that you would resign from the BSA committee. The only person who was allowed to serve on both was Thomasina McKinney.

'It was ultimately a creative relationship. While the interchanges could at times be robust, there was nevertheless an affection underlying them. The BSA has a major focus, which is to declare that their members have to run their business, and this is what it costs to do so. A good example would be the question of fees. When the BSA is making representations to me as chairman of the County Court Rules Committee, who sets the fees and costs for the County Court, I have to go through a regulatory impact study. That is probably a good example of where people are coming from different angles.'

Judge Burgess values local associations

because, generally, they are places where a solicitor can cut his or her teeth in the field of the administration of the profession. He stated:

'I would be hard pressed to think of anyone who became a member of the Law Society council who had not been active previously in the BSA or other local association. This includes many Law Society presidents, including the present one, Donald Eakin, who was BSA president from 1993–4. And I was president of the Law Society in the mid-eighties. There was cross fertilisation. Many BSA people would have been co-opted on to Law Society committees even though we were not on the Law Society council. Nowadays the remit of the Law Society is enormous and sometimes I wonder how they cope, except that the secretariat is excellent.

'The Callender Street Mob [a nickname for solicitors in the early BSA] would have been at its core. Ray Segal, Edwin Gibson, George Palmer – those three together had the capacity to cause wonderfully enormous waves. I laugh at it now with great affection. And when I moved on to the Law Society, sometimes when we were considering an issue and deciding what to do, in the back of your mind lingered the question of what they and the BSA might make of your decision.'

Burgess has always had a keen interest in European and international aspects of legal practice, typified by his appointment as leader of the UK delegation to the Council of Bars and Law Societies of the European Community in the early nineties. In that capacity he was responsible for representing the collective views of the UK legal profession. He dealt with the evolution and negotiation of the seminal Directive on Establishment under Home Title, which allowed, for example, a Belfast solicitor to set up his plate in Paris and vice versa.

Also in the early nineties, Tom Burgess was pioneering a new venture, working as a sole practitioner offering a package of services to other small practices who did not have extensive expertise in company and commercial work.

'I would act for the client who had a

I would be hard pressed to think of anyone who became a member of the Law Society council who had not been active previously in the BSA or other local association.

This portrait of Thomasina (Tommy) McKinney by Lydia de Burgh, HRUA UWS, hangs in the offices of LSNI. Tommy was the only person to serve simultaneously on both the BSA committee and LSNI council. She also became the first female president of the Law Society of Northern Ireland.

LSNI & EWAN HARKNESS

particular transaction, but undertaking, in writing, that I would never work for their client – so that they would never be afraid of losing that client,' he explained. 'We had also put together a package of multi-disciplinary professionals with whom I had worked over the years in commercial and company matters – such as Great Northern Tower, the shopping centre at Holywood Arches, and the Robinson & Cleaver building – to offer a suite of services.'

Then, after he had ceased to be a partner in Tughan & Company and just as his plans for his new practice and offices were at an advanced stage, his appointment to the Bench overtook that aspiration:

'I had been a deputy County Court judge, sitting part-time but regularly on civil work for a couple of years, so I had a fair idea of the judicial function. The decision to accept full-time appointment and to give up other plans which were at an exciting stage was frankly a difficult one. But I have absolutely no regrets about my choice and I am delighted also that we now have three other solicitor colleagues, Judge Derek Rodgers, Judge David McFarland and Judge Philip Babington, serving with such distinction on the County Court Bench.'

The Laganside Courts
complex, Belfast
LISA DYNAN

After his appointment, Judge Burgess became a peripatetic judge, then the Recorder of Londonderry. He remained in post for seven years, until he moved to Belfast and in 2005 was appointed Recorder of Belfast.

'My time in the north-west,' Burgess recalls, 'was invaluable and extremely enjoyable. It is very much the division in which I settled down to the job, learning much about the responsibilities – also the rewards – of managing a diverse caseload, covering civil litigation of all types as well as criminal, family and licensing work.'

The position of Recorder of Belfast has always tended to be regarded de facto as distinctive, if only because the amount of work transacted in Belfast has historically made it the busiest court venue.

In April 2006 a new dimension was added to Judge Burgess's role with his appointment as presiding judge with responsibility for the County Courts. This was part of the restructuring of responsibilities for judicial business under the Justice Act 2004, with presiding judges appointed at each court tier accountable overall to the Lord Chief Justice. Judge Burgess commented:

'It is important to realise that this reorganisation is to do with reinforcing judicial independence under the Lord Chief Justice as head of the judiciary. It does not affect but rather complements the role of individual judges in determining the outcome of individual cases and I am not empowered in any way to inhibit this.

'The practical outworkings of all this is that I remain responsible for the administration of the County Court work in Belfast specifically, but I am also responsible for the delivery of an efficient and timely disposal of the work of the County Courts across Northern Ireland. This involves working with my colleagues to ensure the best allocation of judicial resources, but also to develop good, standardised and consistent working practices and protocols aimed at managing cases from an early stage to hearing or trial. I have other responsibilities in terms of sitting on committees and chairing the aforementioned County Court Rules

Committee. I also have responsibility for working with the Court Service in the running of the Laganside Courts complex, and chair the Users' Committee, comprising a wide range of users of the court building and the court system.'

Judge Burgess confirms that the job he took on when first appointed has changed to a degree which few could have predicted. He points to the fresh emphasis on judicial case-management, and the increasing interest in alternative dispute resolution. He highlights with emphatic approval the development of judicial training under the auspices of the Judicial Studies Board:

'When I started, the concept, let alone the practice of continuous learning for judges was far from recognised. There has been a transformation both in attitude and commitment, so that now I believe it is universally accepted by the judges that we can and should receive regular and systematic updating on all aspects of our work.'

He also refers with conspicuous enthusiasm to the development of IT in the courtroom and in case processing, and as a powerful research tool for the practice and administration of the law. Despite acknowledgement that there are aspects of private practice he continues to miss, Tom Burgess speaks warmly of the working life of the modern judge:

'No matter how important efficient case management and technical aids are to the job, judicial work will always be fundamentally a people business. The intellectual challenge and stimulation are rewarding. While achieving an efficient service will always bring a proper sense of satisfaction, the real work is as a judge and that must always be conducted at a human level. There is nothing as sobering but at the same time as rewarding as discharging, to the best of your ability, responsibilities which you know have a significant impact on the present and future lives of others – victims and defendants – many being vulnerable human beings. This applies whether you are dealing with a finely balanced question of guilt or innocence, length of custodial sentence, or the emotional devastation of

The job Tom Burgess took on when first appointed has changed to a degree which few could have predicted.

Judge Burgess works long hours but gives every appearance of a man who loves his job.

a family break-up and determining the arrangements for children.'

He has clear and well-articulated views on the contribution solicitors can make:

'The public of Northern Ireland is as a rule well served by our solicitors. Access to justice is not just about finance. Access is also about everybody being able to get a solicitor. In a country of a relatively small number of smallish towns – outside two large conurbations – you need a spread of solicitors, easily accessible, near to hand. It is no use telling someone to go to Belfast for a solicitor. That person needs access to someone in whom he or she has confidence, including confidence that the solicitor will act independently and fearlessly in the clients interests.'

Judge Burgess works long hours but gives every appearance of a man who loves his job. His counsel to solicitors is this:

'A judicial career will not be for everyone. Like any job it has its fulfilments and frustrations. But I am an enthusiast by nature, and I think that there has never been a more propitious time for solicitors to consider this as a serious career option. The fact that solicitors are now eligible statutorily for all judicial posts is important and welcome but is only part of the picture. We also have young people, female and male, of ability and tremendous potential, joining the solicitors' ranks, and a Judicial Appointments Commission which is keen to explore ways of maximising the attraction of able candidates. My last word of advice and encouragement to any solicitor would be, if you get a chance to serve in a judicial capacity, whether full- or part-time, take it! The prospect may be a little scary, but you never know where you may end up.'

Tom Burgess has ended up a long way from his days as a BSA chairman holding committee gatherings in his own home, where, 'if you were early you got the sofa. If you were late, you ended up on the dining room chair.'

OUR INDEPENDENCE IS UNDER ATTACK

Michael Davey

Michael Davey was chairman of the BSA from 1981–2 and is a past secretary of the Law Society of Northern Ireland.

Shortly before leaving the Law Society in 1996 I was asked to speculate as to what the profession might expect to experience over the course of the coming years. I said then that we had to look at the quality of what we do and how we deliver it, since quality, not price, had to be our selling point.

At that time the Law Society had been trying to help the profession adapt to change by improving standards, reviewing work methods and responding to the needs of clients. I foresaw the advent of compulsory professional development and suggested that the Society and the Disciplinary Tribunal would have to look harder at the systems for producing competence and for rooting out incompetence. I suggested that they could improve quality by helping each other, perhaps by way of approved consultancy or referral arrangements, or by some kind of society provision, in the same manner as had been established in the financial services field.

Another way I suggested for improving quality was copying, in other areas, the example of the Home Charter scheme, where a somewhat basic attempt to define professional standards had been made. By setting out what was expected, and by appropriate accreditation, actual standards could be expected to improve. In commercial terms it might be called establishing and marketing the brand.

At about the same time, Judge David Edward of the European Court of First Instance was talking of a new heresy, that the practice of law is a business like any other commercial activity. While believing in the value of learning from the world of commerce, I shared his concern. My particular concern here was with the

independence of the profession and with the much misunderstood problem of conflict of interest.

These areas of concern arose partly from the pressures to which the profession had already been subjected in the 1980s and partly from the way governments and government organisations were talking in the mid-1990s. During the 1980s there had been a variety of proposals, including the extension of rights in the conveyancing field to banks, building societies and licensed conveyancers; the opening up of advocacy rights to unqualified persons; the extension of probate practice to banks; and the introduction of multidisciplinary partnerships and outside ownership of firms.

We had also been subjected to what was wholly inaccurately described as the deregulation of financial services. By the 1990s various government figures had made it clear that they regarded the function of professional bodies as being to ensure, firstly, that the standards of competence and professional conduct among practitioners gave adequate protection for clients and, secondly, that their services were provided both economically and efficiently. It seemed likely, therefore, that there would be greater scrutiny of the Society's efforts in those directions and a greater willingness on the part of government to contemplate the possibility that if the profession was

no longer doing these things satisfactorily, someone else could be introduced to do them instead.

These concerns were not misplaced. Scrutiny did take place in England through the Office of Fair Trading. It was not wholly surprising, given the position in England at the time, that its report was critical. In response to this report, the government appointed Sir David Clementi, the former deputy governor of the Bank of England, to carry out an independent review of the regulation of legal services in England and Wales. A number of major reforms were proposed, with the likely impact on the profession ranging from significant discomfort to excruciating pain. The suggestions included a new Legal Services Board to oversee the work of all legal service providers with a mechanism separating the representative and regulatory roles of the Law Society; a new independent and freestanding office for legal complaints removing the complaints handling process from the profession entirely; and, finally, a recommendation that lawyers from different professional bodies be free to form partnerships together in what Clementi called legal disciplinary practices. He also recommended that non-lawyers should be permitted to be involved in the management and ownership of these practices, though even he stopped short of recommending that multidisciplinary practices, to include professions other than lawyers, should be legalised in view of the obvious regulatory

difficulties. The government was not so restrained. It accepted all the recommendations and extended the proposed legislation to include multidisciplinary practices.

It was not to be expected that, having cast the cold eye of review over the legal profession in England and Wales, the government would neglect to do the same for Northern Ireland. It is always difficult when a firm decision has been taken on policy for one region to argue, particularly in a direct rule situation, that another region should be treated differently. This was the problem which faced the profession here at the end of 2005 when the Legal Services Review Group under the chairmanship of Professor Sir George Bain was established. The task for the profession was to persuade the Review Group that there should be a Northern Irish solution to a Northern Irish problem and that the recommendations which had been adopted so enthusiastically for England and Wales should not be adopted wholesale here.

It was a big ask. The Society was equal to the challenge and did an outstanding job. The Review Body reported and proposed that the legal profession should continue to discharge their regulatory functions without separating them from their representative functions. The present role of the Chief Justice in relation to professional rules should become advisory and a new Legal Services Oversight Commissioner should audit professional rules and oversee the operations of the professions themselves. A greater degree of involvement for lay people in the complaints process is recommended, but, again, responsibility for complaints is to remain with the profession. A power to award limited compensation, capped at the level of the excess on the current professional negligence policy, was suggested. Finally no change is proposed on the creation of inter-legal partnerships or multidisciplinary practices.

These proposals are wholly consistent with the government objectives previously described and which were largely repeated, at greater length, by Clementi, but they recognise the differences in scale,

It Was Like This Your Worship
Albert Walmsley

At that time most of the solicitors did their own cases in the county court and addressed the juries themselves. Indeed, two of the older practitioners would sometimes join together in one case. One would address the jury and the other would do the cross-examination, but that practice died out towards the beginning of the war and is now almost unheard of, which is a pity in a way as there were some very good advocates in the solicitors' profession. They were particularly good at dealing with juries because a solicitor would see more people in the course of a year's practice than a barrister would see in five or ten years, so the solicitor tended to know much more about people, how they lived and thought and what their various prejudices were.

in the history of regulation by the profession and in the nature and structure of the profession in Northern Ireland as compared to England.

But what of the future? We must continue to fight for the independence of the profession. The profession's independence is, as the history of the past twenty years has shown, under attack in two principal ways. The first is the attack on self-regulation and the second is the underestimating of the problem of conflict of interest. Self-regulation is a privilege. It is viewed with jealousy by others and should be equally jealously guarded. Sometimes people ask whether it would matter if we lost the power to regulate ourselves. Of course it would matter. It would matter a lot. It is suggested that if we were deregulated we would no longer be confined by regulations and that we would be relieved of all the associated costs. This is pie in the sky. There is no possibility of a choice between self regulation and no regulation. Deregulation does not mean an absence of regulation; it means the substitution of regulation by ourselves with regulation by other people; other people who know nothing of the problems faced by solicitors and who would not care even if they did. Regulation by other people who would have no interest in the legal profession and who would be concerned only with the ticking of their own boxes and the meeting of their own targets. Regulation by other people who would not be subject to any significant budgetary restraint and who would be unconcerned by the weight and cost of the regulatory burden on the profession since they would not have to bear it. They would not be spending their own money, but ours.

Anyone who thinks deregulation is cheap should enquire from the financial services industry how cheap they found it to be. Solicitors will still have to be educated, they will still have to be licensed, they will still have to carry insurance, they will still have to keep accounts, they will still be subject to complaint. The willingness of government to become involved in all or any of these areas has become progressively more apparent in the last twenty-five years. There is no evidence that that willingness is going to disappear. Government involvement in any of these processes will not appear in the shape of a welfare benefit but as a punitive tax.

The other area of attack on the profession's independence relates to conflict of interest, a concept little understood outside the profession itself. There is a modern tendency to believe that so long as the client is aware that his advisor's interests are in conflict with his own there is no problem. Anyone who doubts this should re-read the proposals made years ago for the extension of the right to carry out conveyancing to the building societies or should remember that it took over twenty years for the Financial Services Authority to understand that you cannot really call yourself an independent financial advisor if you are only selling the products of one financial provider and selling these on commission. This is an area of particular concern, especially proposals already suggested which would enable law firms to be owned by persons other than lawyers or, to put it another way, which would enable lawyers to give advice to their employer's customers.

The Bar Council said in its evidence to the Bain Review: 'A legal practice which is run for the final benefit of its external investors/shareholders would come to have very different values and a very different culture from that which is the norm in legal practices today.' Neatly put. It would also have a profound effect on the manner in which legal services would be delivered to the public. The major providers of legal services could become supermarkets, insurance companies, banks and other financial behemoths. It is questionable whether the full effects of such a change on the availability of legal services and the nature of the services which would be provided have been thought through fully or at all.

Similar reservations apply to multidisciplinary practices and, particularly, the manner of controlling and regulating them. It is essential that the objectivity and independence of legal

Deregulation does not mean an absence of regulation; it means the substitution of regulation by ourselves with regulation by other people.

One would hope to see the First Minister and Deputy First Minister being invited and welcomed to the new Law Society House.

advice should be maintained. A client is entitled to know that the advice that he is getting is directed towards the furtherance of his interests and his interests alone. That is the kind of independence clients look for and it is the confidence in that kind of objectivity which makes clients want to buy the lawyer's services. In the final analysis that objectivity, otherwise known as our professional honour, is what we have to sell.

If that is what we have to fight against, how do we go about it? On a strategic level we need only to remind ourselves of what regulation is for: namely, to ensure that the standard of competence and conduct in the profession is adequate to protect the clients and that the profession's services are widely available and provided efficiently. That is the basis on which the Society's representational and promotional activities have to be based, a further

reason, if one were needed, for self-regulation. Maintain standards, retain objectivity and the corporate reputation of the profession will be high. On a more practical level it has to be remembered that, in the last analysis, changes to the profession's structure require political action. It is important therefore to be aware of what is in the political air, to be able to influence the direction in which the political will is travelling or, at the very least, to be able to influence the manner and route by which the final political destination is reached. To that end one would hope to see the First Minister and Deputy First Minister being invited and welcomed to the new Law Society House on a regular basis and the Society's officers and staff being familiar to and familiar with the persons behind the various doors in the corridors of power.

Open bottle, shut case
ROD FRIERS

It Was Like This Your Worship   Albert Walmsley

While making my submission in court I made the point that no one had proved that the sample before the court was poteen. I lifted the bottle, pulled out the cork and put the cork on the table in front of me. The liquid on the cork cleaned the varnish off the table down to the bare wood. And bang went the last arguable point in the case.

TO BE WANTED AND RESPECTED

Brian Garrett

Brian Garrett is a senior consultant with Elliott Duffy Garrett, Belfast. He is an arbitrator, deputy County Court judge and a life-sentence commissioner. He is currently chairman of the Tyrone Guthrie Centre, Annaghmakerrig, County Monaghan, and was president of the Irish Association and a visiting associate fellow (International Affairs) at Harvard University.

If, as a profession, we respond to the needs of society and show by our practice and thinking we have a socially relevant and helpful contribution to make to the management and regulation of our society as it prepares to enter the twenty-first century, we shall be wanted and respected.

SIR LESLIE SCARMAN
English Law: The New Dimension

This challenge, identified more than thirty years ago by the late Lord Scarman, and the formula he identified for a successful outcome, merit consideration. It is a challenge which lawyers should not shirk, while acknowledging that the ultimate decision on the outcome must lie with the general public. It may be appropriate to suggest that the issue has particular relevance for solicitors today in Northern Ireland, not least in the context of the new, post-Belfast Agreement constitutional arrangements.

When I was invited to contribute this essay, it was suggested that it would be timely to assess what the legal profession in Northern Ireland can reasonably claim to have learned and achieved in terms of their Troubles experience, and how effectively they coped with the strains of this period. These matters do not admit of a simple, let alone a generally agreed response and so it is with some diffidence (and the knowledge that there are others whose experience is such that they could respond more convincingly than me) that the following limited observations are made.

Assuming there could be created an accurate, evidential weighing-machine designed to measure success and failure of solicitors in Northern Ireland since 1969, it would be my contention that the balance of the weight of such evidence would be

found, and to a significant degree, on the success side of the scale. No doubt in the period ahead a number of detailed studies and surveys will be produced dealing with various aspects of this topic and one can anticipate that the relevant material will be able to be analysed in a comprehensive manner. But while making no claim in this essay for depth of analysis or objectivity, I would highlight the following as representing some of the most telling arguments that support the contention that success was achieved.

First, the remarkable record of the Northern Ireland judiciary throughout the post-1969 period in demonstrating commitment to the rule of law, and in exercising judicial independence (all this despite sustained threats throughout the period to their personal safety, with tragic consequences for a number of the judiciary who lost their lives). Then the increasing tendency of the general public in Northern Ireland during this period to resort to legal process in securing their rights, with support from both branches of the legal profession – solicitors and barristers – in doing so. And, finally, the underlying unity and sense of purpose which were able to be maintained by the members of each branch of the legal profession in Northern Ireland. In mentioning the threat that was posed to the judiciary it is also right to recall that there were other members of the legal profession who suffered threat and injury (one is here reminded of the murders, in controversial circumstances, of Patrick Finucane and Rosemary Nelson, both well-known solicitors involved in criminal law defence work).

It is not now suggested that *all* of the evidence lies on the success side of the scale, even if this is the side which is heavily weighted. The critical features outlined above as underpinning overall success should not serve to justify an excess of self-congratulation, nor should they obscure such shortcomings as did occur. The factor that provided the context for the suggested successful outcome can, ultimately, be attributed to the maintenance of civic life by the security forces, and the work of all those who in their daily lives rejected inter-community conflict. This maintenance of civic life (constrained as it was from time to time) proved costly in terms of lives as well as money, and was achieved in no small part due to the innate good sense and restraint of the majority of people in the wider community.

It would also be misleading to paint a picture of a legal profession that was not disturbed by events or to suggest that solicitors as individuals were not divided in their view of particular events. Solicitors in Northern Ireland, as elsewhere, are not produced in flat-pack IKEA form. They are a diverse group holding a range of individual views on political and other issues. It would be foolish to suggest that there was no occasion when such differences of view, if unchecked, might not find the profession divided along sectarian lines. It is noteworthy that when it came to the expression of the overall professional view, both the Law Society of Northern Ireland and the Northern Ireland Bar Council spoke effectively and responsibly for all their members and did so by concentrating on the well-tried code of conduct which solicitors traditionally are expected to honour.

For solicitors, two principles of professional conduct/ethics provided, and continue to provide the essential guidance, namely:

Solicitors Practice Rule 1 (Basic Principles)

A solicitor shall not do anything in the course of practising as a solicitor, or permit another person to do anything on his or her behalf, which compromises or impairs or is likely to compromise or impair any of the following:
(a) the solicitor's independence or integrity;
(b) a person's freedom to instruct a solicitor of his or her choice;
(c) the solicitor's duty to act in the best interests of the client;
(d) the good repute of the solicitor or of the solicitors' profession;
(e) the solicitor's proper standard of work;
(f) the solicitor's duty to the Court.

International Bar Association International Code of Ethics

(2) Lawyers shall at all times maintain the honour and dignity of their profession. They shall in practice, as well as in private life, abstain from any behaviour which may tend to discredit the profession of which they are members.
(3) Lawyers shall preserve independence in the discharge of their professional duty.

The above sets demanding standards. These principles do not, however, assume that solicitors as individuals should be detached from controversial society debate, or be expected to adopt the famed 'Three Monkeys' negative formula when it comes to matters of seeing, hearing or doing. Solicitors, like others, remain free to express their views as individuals, provided that in doing so they do not cross the line in a manner which is calculated to jeopardise the proper discharge of their professional duty.

It should be remembered that solicitors in Northern Ireland enjoy some distinct advantages, which are of immense benefit in their dealings with each other and the

A further question that is prompted is whether solicitors in Northern Ireland can be reasonably satisfied that … they have adequately demonstrated commitment to a non-sectarian ethos?

community. First, they are the custodians of well-tested and powerful legal traditions. Solicitors as officers of the court will be conscious of the responsibility this entails. Secondly, and not insignificantly, most practising solicitors in Northern Ireland have in the course of their training been a member of a wider (student) body drawn from various sections of society, and so they will have formed genuine bonds of respect for and friendship with one another – an experience which proves invaluable in later professional life.

Some other questions are prompted. How well, for example, have solicitors in Northern Ireland fared when judged against the above principles of professional conduct, and how effectively have they utilised their advantages? Answers to these questions will again be best left to the decision of others. A further question that is prompted is whether solicitors in Northern Ireland can be reasonably satisfied that within their own respective offices, and generally in their professional life, they have adequately demonstrated commitment to a non-sectarian ethos? Thus, is the office staff composition one that reflects different traditions within the wider community? Again, when briefing counsel, do solicitors routinely issue instructions to members of the Bar based solely on merit (assuming availability)? Are particular clients encouraged to believe their solicitor actually supports their views and actions (no matter how questionable), as opposed to their solicitor being confined to the energetic expression of clients' legal rights? To pose such questions may seem tiresome and in some cases may risk a response along the lines of 'Oh, yes, all very worthy, but it's not that easy in the real world.' Maybe – and there can be little doubt that there are areas and conditions of practice that are particularly problematic, and that solicitors whose principle work is in the field of criminal law inevitably carry the main burden.

At the time of writing this essay it is not yet certain whether the arrangements for devolved powers to the Northern Ireland Assembly and Executive will prove durable, but the signs are relatively reassuring. In the present way of things, devolution of powers within the main regions of the United Kingdom is generally favoured, and there are strong forces, both nationally and internationally, favouring the current arrangements (with or without adjustment, but leaving intact the central plank of inter-community government). Currently, a major issue is whether jurisdiction over police and justice is to be devolved to Northern Ireland, and the balance of the evidence would suggest that this will occur in the not too distant future. The devolution of police and justice powers in turn will bring new issues for the legal profession in Northern Ireland.

In the context of devolution, a question mark will hang over whether law reform in Northern Ireland will reflect (as has been the case) corresponding measures of reform in other parts of the United Kingdom, or whether devolution will tend to promote resort to local measures unconnected in character to other parts of the United Kingdom. This is an important issue and a balance will need to be achieved. Now that Northern Ireland has its own (statutory) law reform machinery, it will be interesting to learn which route law reform philosophy will follow.

So the scene is set for change, and whatever the outcome so far as devolution is concerned, many areas of law may be expected to grow in complexity, which will in turn throw up new challenges for the practitioner. Thus the current expansion of the role of judicial review is unlikely to be curbed. Environmental and social security law are marked for significant growth. Data information demands and concern for privacy will continue and may be presumed to result in new legal measures. Human rights law will grow apace and the cases in which human rights issues are raised can be expected to increase with the underlying arguments becoming more complex and creative. All this, and much more no doubt, will occur while the main body of civil and criminal law will also undergo change.

The need for legal services of high quality over an ever wider range of subjects can be expected to create testing

A question mark will hang over whether law reform in Northern Ireland will ... promote resort to local measures unconnected in character to other parts of the United Kingdom.

demands so far as the legal profession is concerned, but there is reason to be confident that this can be met even if competition for the provision of legal services becomes greater. It is against this background that solicitors in Northern Ireland will have welcomed the thrust of Professor Sir George Bain's Legal Services Review Board recommendations which, while seeking changes in the regulatory and complaints-handling aspects governing solicitors, firmly rejected blanket endorsement of various features of the corresponding Clementi Review for England and Wales ('Review of the Regulatory Framework for Legal Services in England and Wales', December 2004), which in turn led to the subsequent government White Paper and proposals to permit external ownership of law firms.

There are, as well, new and vigorous forces at hand in the bid to secure a successful outcome to Lord Scarman's challenge, cited at the head of this essay. One important but not adequately recognised factor is the increasing number of talented women who have entered both branches of the legal profession over the past twenty years, and who have done so in a profession which traditionally has been less than a bastion of gender equality. This is a radical development and one which not only changes the profile of the profession, but also the range and depth of its interests and influence.

The legal profession has, of course, become all too used to uncomplimentary remarks. There is no reason to lose heart. Consider and reject, for example, the jaundiced slur which the protagonist of Swift's *Gulliver's Travels* puts forward:

Here my Master interposing, said, 'it was a Pity, that Creatures endowed with such prodigious Abilities of Mind, as these Lawyers, by the Description I gave of them, must certainly be, were not rather encouraged to be Instructors of others in Wisdom and Knowledge.' In Answer to which I assured his Honour, 'that in all Points out of their own Trade, they were usually the most ignorant and stupid Generation among us, the most despicable in common Conversation,

avowed Enemies to all Knowledge and Learning, and equally disposed to pervert the general Reason of Mankind in every other Subject of Discourse as in that of their own Profession.'

Finally, a footnote which may be of some relevance when advising future entrants to the profession. Every lawyer from time to time is asked for advice as to whether a particular young person should consider following a career in law and, if so, what would be the best basis for doing so. If pressed, one would have difficulty in bettering the advice given in 1954 by the great Justice Felix Frankfurter to a twelve-year-old Paul Claussen Jr:

My dear Paul

No one can be a truly competent lawyer unless he is a cultivated man. If I were you, I would forget all about any technical preparation for the law. The best way to prepare for the law is to come to the study of the law as a well-read person. Thus alone can one acquire the capacity to use the English language on paper and in speech and with the habits of clear thinking which only a truly liberal education can give. No less important for a lawyer is the cultivation of the imaginative faculties by reading poetry, seeing great paintings, in the original or in easily available reproductions, and listening to great music. Stock your mind with the deposit of much good reading, and widen and deepen your feelings by experiencing vicariously as much as possible the wonderful mysteries of the universe, and forget all about your future career.

    With good wishes,
    Sincerely yours,

    Felix Frankfurter

Justice Frankfurter's advice stands the test of time and, if followed, a career in law can be expected to look after itself, and, with it, the respect which Lord Scarman identified as necessary for the legal profession to win will be assured.

Every lawyer from time to time is asked for advice as to whether a particular young person should consider following a career in law.

The BSA and
LAW REFORM

Neil Faris

Neil Faris is a solicitor commissioner for the Northern Ireland Law Commission and was chairman of the Belfast Solicitors' Association from 1986–7.

Among the objects of the Belfast Solicitors' Association as set out in its constitution is that the Association is 'to take such steps as are available to the Association to ensure the provision of ethical and efficient legal services to the community in Belfast'.

I have been a member of the Association since the late 1970s, and was closely involved as committee member and office bearer in the 1980s. Drawing on my memories and the available records of the Association, I think it is worthwhile to review how, in terms of law reform, the Association has measured up to the obligations of its constitution. I conclude with some brief personal thoughts on the role of the Association in the future in relation to the recent launch of the Law Commission for Northern Ireland (with a statutory, independent role for law reform in this jurisdiction). As indicated, I do not do this wearing my Law Reform hat, but as a continuing member of the Association, with the hope that it may continue its enthusiastic and activist role in these affairs.

As with any aspect of the history of affairs in Northern Ireland, one must sing of old unhappy far off things and battles long ago. But I hope I do so in as constructive and objective way so far as I can. Certainly, the past thirty years are littered with attempts by government to reform the professions of solicitors and barristers and under direct rule these initiatives have extended to Northern Ireland. The Association has participated in the defence of the professions. But that has not been an uncritical defence. There have been spats of disagreement or contention over the years both with the Bar of Northern Ireland and even with the Law Society of Northern Ireland, the

governing body for solicitors throughout Northern Ireland.

In the beginning, then, was the Benson Commission, which was appointed by the government of Harold Wilson in 1976 as the first of these attempts to reform the practices and governance arrangements of the legal professions. I remember as a solicitor's apprentice being asked rather anxiously by one of the partners in the law firm where I worked did I think there would be a future in these reforms. Of course, my legal education at the time had not lead me to any degree of interest in these matters of pressing concern to my seniors, who were especially apprehensive about the preservation of the conveyancing monopoly and the threat of enforced fusion of the solicitors and barristers into one profession.

In the event, the mighty labours of the Benson Commission over a three-year period ended with its report issued in 1979. But there was little practical impact – at least from the perspective of ordinary legal practitioners. However, although (or perhaps because) the threat of fusion of solicitors and barristers had gone away, in the 1980s the Association pursued a reform initiative on its own against certain practices of the Bar Library, which in the view of the Association were less than conducive to the provision of efficient legal services to the community in Belfast. This led to almost open hostilities between the Association and the Bar at the time of the next governmental initiative for reform of the legal professions. In

January 1989, the Lord Chancellor Lord Mackay published a series of Green Papers seeking to root out the perceived anti-competitive practices of both professions (part of the free market-philosophy of the governments of Margaret Thatcher).

There had, in fact, been a (rare) meeting at the beginning of January 1989 between representatives of the Law Society, of the Association (including myself) and of the Bar (including Brian Kerr QC, now Lord Chief Justice of Northern Ireland, and Declan Morgan, then barrister at law and now judge of the High Court and Chair of the Northern Ireland Law Commission). That meeting was held in the shadow of the impending issue of the Green Papers, and it ended with discussion about liaison between the professions in their responses to the Green Papers. But while on the one hand, the Association's representatives made clear their continuing unhappiness with the

administrative arrangements at the Bar Library, on the other, this was not accepted nor conceded by the Bar's representatives.

In August 1989 the Association set out in detail their points of view in the Response by the BSA to the Green Papers (and to a Northern Ireland Supplement which had been issued by the direct rule administration in May 1989). The Association's Response challenged in detail the then current Bar Library arrangements and this provoked a Reply (undated, but issued in 1990) from the Bar, followed by a Rejoinder by the Association to the Bar in October 1990. Whether any of that had any effect on government's thinking remains open to doubt. In the event, it took the direct rule administration until July 1991 to issue a White Paper, 'Legal Services for Northern Ireland', proposing wide-ranging reforms, including the introduction of (non-solicitor) 'authorised conveyancing practitioners'. The intention was to apply in Northern Ireland reforms that had been introduced in England and Wales in the Courts and Legal Services Act 1990. This provoked energetic campaigning by the Law Society, supported by the Association, leading to a Special General Meeting of the Law Society on 18 September 1991. The Law Society then introduced the Home Charter quality standard to be observed by all solicitors in residential conveyancing transactions and it appears that this satisfied the government not to impose further measures on the solicitors' profession here.

In the event, the relationship between the Association and the Bar fortunately did not break down and a degree of liaison continued in following years. It is right, also, to acknowledge some substantial reforms since then initiated by the Bar itself, including its splendid Bar Library, which graces the corner of Victoria Street. And the modern technological advances of fax, voicemail and email have done so much to improve communications between members of the two professions. (Communication problems were at the heart of our grievances with the Bar at the time.) But I

The Bar Library, Belfast
LISA DYNAN

do hope that today's Association will remain alert to taking up any matters where it perceives shortfall.

The Association's website, www.belfast-solicitors-association.org, refers to its long history of involvement with the Law Society, with many committee members of the Association serving on the Law Society's subcommittees and council, and in many cases going on to become presidents of the Law Society. But the Association has always jealously guarded its independence and has been prepared to take its own view on proposed legislation and procedures where it cannot accept the Law Society position. This came to the fore in the preparations for the next attempt by government to reform the legal professions in Northern Ireland. After the excitement of late 1991, for the remainder of that decade and well into this decade there was peace on that front. But this was broken in September 2005 when the Department of Finance and Personnel (at the time under direct rule control) issued a consultation document, The Regulation of Legal Services in Northern Ireland. This proposed the introduction into Northern Ireland of the Clementi Reforms, which were being applied in England and Wales. These, following a report by Sir David Clementi, entailed fundamental change to the governance arrangements for the Law Society in England and Wales, which separated out its regulatory functions from its representative role.

In fact, in Northern Ireland the Association had, over the years, evinced increasing concern about the way the Law Society here was running. It had particularly taken up the issue from 1993 onwards, and had raised, at its annual meeting with the Law Society President, its concern as to whether in carrying the dual role of regulator and representative body the Law Society was in fact adequately defending solicitors' legitimate interests. But the Association was at one with the Law Society that there should be no reform which would lead to any form (direct or indirect) of governmental control over the legal professions in Northern Ireland. In the event, the

November 2006 report of the Legal Services Review Group, led by Professor Sir George Bain, largely endorsed the continuance of both regulatory and representative roles in the current governance arrangements for both branches of the legal profession in Northern Ireland. In particular, the Review Group was satisfied that there was no evidence of breakdown of the complaints and discipline systems applying to solicitors in Northern Ireland. (The Law Society of England and Wales appeared to have endemic problems in these areas, which had necessitated the Clementi reforms.)

The Bain report does, however, recommend some significant changes, in particular a lay-majority on the complaints and disciplinary committees of both professions, and the appointment of an independent Legal Services Oversight Commissioner. These recommendations have not yet appeared in legislation. But given the restoration of devolution, this now falls to the Northern Ireland Executive and Assembly. No doubt the Association will play its active part in that process, and whether our local politicians will be content to accept the recommendations of the Bain report (from the direct rule era) remains to be seen. Possibly a new role for the Association is to consider how to use the new opportunities that devolution affords to ensure the ethical provision of legal services. That objective also applies to the work of the Association with law reform generally, as well as to the reform initiatives for the legal profession.

Among the Association's quite extensive archives, the secretary's report on the year 1985/6 survives. Apart from being my own handiwork, I feel it is interesting in demonstrating the wide scope of the Association's involvement in law reform matters. The report lists the involvement of the Association in the following areas:

- A visit from Professor Desmond Greer, then dean of the Law Faculty of Queen's University, to discuss in a personal capacity 'the question of legal

The Association was at one with the Law Society that there should be no reform which would lead to any form of governmental control over the legal professions in Northern Ireland.

education about which the Committee remains seriously concerned'. This related to proposals for the reform of the Institute of Professional Legal Studies which came to a head in the following year.

- A meeting with Thomas A. Burgess (now Judge Burgess) as chairman of the Professional Indemnity Subcommittee of the Law Society and Mr Tom McGrath, 'the insurance broker', to discuss the Master Policy for Solicitors Professional Indemnity Insurance. The particular concern of the BSA committee was recorded in relation to 'the high level of claims and an alleged lack of cooperation on the part of solicitors in giving early notification of claims and in dealing with claims'.

- The Law Society president (Mr Turkington) and the secretary (Mr Davey) attended the May meeting of the committee. 'The discussion covered in particular professional and continuing education, advertising and conveyancing packages, the Law Society Handbook and costs directions, Department of the Environment Vesting Costs, relationship with the Bar of Northern Ireland and the administration of the Law Society.' Some perennial topics feature in that list.

- Mr Alan Burnside, the public relations consultant of the Law Society, attended the June meeting 'to discuss the projected image building by the Law Society and by the profession in general'. This was in the early days of the profession beginning to recognise that it had to present its case to the public.

Then follows a list of agenda items dealt with by the committee in the course of the year including:

- representations to the Enforcement of Judgments Review Committee
- problems of civil legal aid
- 'conveyancing packages'
- the relationship with the Bar 'as the Committee considers the present

arrangements for dealing with barristers to be completely unsatisfactory'
- costs issues with the Crown solicitor, the Housing Executive and the Department of the Environment
- the delay in obtaining property certificates

The report also notes the then novel proposal of some rural Associations that Vendors should supply these Certificates and considered the matter further but has decided not to support any change at least in present circumstances'. This change was, however, later introduced by way of the Law Society Home Charter for residential conveyancing.

The Report then records the activities of the Association that year including:

- contributions to *The Writ*, the recently introduced house magazine of the Law Society
- a BSA stand at the Ideal Home Exhibition
- considering advertising in the Thursday property pages of the *Belfast Telegraph*

The Association also receives, on a regular basis, proposals for legislation and consultation documents for comment from various government departments. In the year 1985/6 these included:

- the draft Enduring Powers of Attorney Order
- the proposed draft Rates Amendment Order
- the European Community Regulation on European Economic Interest Group
- 'various drafts remain under consideration'

The report also records the Association's representation on other bodies: the Belfast Law Centre (now Law Centre (NI)), the Duty Solicitor Scheme, the Land Registry Liaison Committee and the Law Society Subcommittee for Tribunals.

The committee opted to continue the Association's well-established involvement in continuing legal education, but 'had decided to experiment with a one-day seminar course and will engage Messrs Lowe & Gordon Seminars from London'. One novel proposal was a Belfast City Centre Partnership – 'a promotional scheme for professional firms in Belfast city centre and members will be circulated with details of the scheme'.

This is but a snapshot of one year's activities of the Association from over two decades ago. Since then, of course, the Association has driven forward with acquisition of its own office premises and support staff. This recognises that all of its various activities can no longer be reliant upon the voluntary time of officers and members of the Association.

What then for the future? Among the Association's archives can also be found my handwritten notes of the chairman's address to the AGM, held in the Lecture Room of Law Society House, Victoria Street, Belfast, at 5.15 p.m. on Thursday 12 November 1987. I see that among other important matters (such as the dinner with the Dublin Solicitors Bar Association and the golf outing), I spoke of matters of 'representation/reform' which should be undertaken by the Association. I spoke of what I – perhaps dismissively – described as the 'second-hand' systems for law reform then pertaining in Northern Ireland. I specifically complained that we had no Law Commission here, though I noted the initiative of the Law Society

which led to the formation of the Law Reform Advisory Committee – the predecessor to the Northern Ireland Law Commission.

Now some twenty years on there can be no more complaints of 'second-hand'. We have our own Law Commission and a restored system of devolution. So not only is there a new agenda and a new role for the Belfast Solicitors' Association in law reform, there are also new opportunities for contact, representation and work with the new, devolved institutions of the Northern Ireland Executive and the Northern Ireland Assembly (and its various committees), and with the Northern Ireland Law Commission.

I very much hope that the Belfast Solicitors' Association will be to the fore in the legal profession in Northern Ireland; in taking and running with the new opportunities in the interests of members of the Association; in the maintenance of the independence of the legal profession in serving the public; and in the 'pursuit of ethical and efficient legal services to the community in Belfast'.

This is a personal contribution, being some reflections of Neil Faris's experiences as a member and officer of the Belfast Solicitors' Association. The views expressed accordingly are not to be attributed to the Northern Ireland Law Commission.

> Now some twenty years on there can be no more complaints of 'second-hand'. We have our own Law Commission and a restored system of devolution.

Recollections
Donal McFerran

It was a busy day in the custody court, where I was sitting as Deputy Resident Magistrate, with many solicitors anxious to have their case dealt with. A number of the busiest solicitors were darting in and out of court seeing clients and checking on the position of their cases in the other courts. The 'King of the Pettys' Paddy Donnelly had several cases in the list. His first case was called but Mr Donnelly was not present. The case was passed and we continued down the list. Mr Donnelly appeared and was advised his case had been passed. He then disappeared again. His second case was called and duly passed. Some time later I saw his head come round the door and disappear yet again. Then his third case was called and still no sign of Mr Donnelly. Patience was wearing thin at this point and I pondered aloud, 'I wonder would it be possible to secure the presence of Mr Donnelly by issuing a bench warrant.' On hearing this, Jonathan Taylor (no mean court hopper himself) sprang to his feet to announce 'Speaking for myself and my colleagues, I can assure your worship, we would be very grateful if your worship would adopt that very course.' I managed to restrain myself from referring to people in glasshouses. Needless to say, Mr Donnelly was more than a little puzzled by all the wide grins that greeted him when he finally appeared.

'IS THIS A PRACTICAL JOKE?'
A life in practice

Colin Gowdy

Colin Gowdy is a senior partner in King and Gowdy. He was BSA chairman from 1976–7.

I was schooled at Inst, then in the Queen's University Belfast Law Faculty, and when I graduated the first task was to find a master who would take me as an apprentice on the Law Society rolls. In 1967 Tom King, senior partner of S. & R. Crymble of Mayfair Buildings in Arthur Square, accepted me.

Another partner in the firm was Harry McKibbin, father of the present Harry. Tom was a very well-known solicitor in Belfast and a past president of the Law Society. In those days an apprentice was required to sign written indentures. In the indentures that I signed I promised, among other things, to keep the secrets of Thomas King, something which I have done to this day.

I was paid a salary. Although a small amount, it was about the going rate at the time. I was fortunate to receive anything. I remember a colleague telling me that he was introduced by Professor Montrose to Brian Rankin with the aim of becoming his apprentice. Brian Rankin said he was prepared to waive the premium. My colleague's father didn't know what he was talking about. But as late as the fifties and early sixties, paying a premium to the master was the norm, say about £300, which was quite a lot of money. This was to cover the three-year apprenticeship. In later years, the master did not keep the money, but paid it in dribs and drabs to the apprentice during his apprenticeship.

This old process did its job in training the next generation of solicitors, but it did mean that it would have been difficult for people from poorer backgrounds to enter the profession. Indeed, there used to be quite restrictive practices regarding entry to the profession. I was told, for example, that at one stage in history, the solicitors in Omagh got together, all of them, and resolved that anyone who was not related to an existing solicitor could not be employed by any of them!

Mayfair Buildings in Arthur Square was probably built about the turn of the twentieth century. It was aimed at solicitors and allied professions, because the core of the building consisted of strongrooms, which are where solicitors would have kept his clients' title deeds and wills. Mayfair Buildings was a warren of solicitors. S. & R. Crymble was always keen to keep ahead of the technology and one day, somewhere in the late sixties, in came a Rank Xerox photocopier.

The machine was huge and nothing like today's machines. The running costs were quite high. However, the more the machine was used, the cheaper was the unit price of the copies. Modern entrants to the profession may not appreciate what a big advance the compact desktop photocopier actually represents. For centuries, even millennia, copying documents had been a problem that had only partly been solved by the time of the Second World War.

To make the investment in the revolutionary Xerox photocopier more viable, we decided that we would set up the big photocopier in a small office for the use of the nearby offices, with an honesty box beside it. Those in the Mayfair Buildings using the machine would put money in the box according to usage, a system that worked very well. This photocopier was one of the very early machines of its type – indeed, the first plain paper copier – and you had to put black toner powder into it, which was heated up in the copying process to be applied to the paper to form the copy.

One of the users was a well-known solicitor, R.B. Uprichard, known to all and sundry as Buster. He was, at the time, the Crown Solicitor for Antrim and one of his functions was the preparation of the paperwork for County Antrim trials at Crumlin Road Courthouse.

Before the advent of the photocopier, he had been using a typewriter with multiple sheets of paper interlaced with multiple sheets of carbon paper to make copies of the relevant papers for the judge, senior counsel for the prosecution and senior counsel for the defence and the juniors, the solicitors and so forth. You can easily imagine that with the number of copies that was required, the last

carbon copy on the last sheet of paper was normally scarcely readable. So the advent of the Rank Xerox machine was a godsend for Buster.

Buster had more of a broad, fresh approach. Detail was something that could be left until later. On one particular day there was an important trial at Crumlin Road. The presiding judge was the then Lord Chief Justice, Lord MacDermott. Buster handed a sheaf of papers up to the bench. The Lord Chief Justice examined them, becoming redder and redder in the face as he leafed though the sheets of paper.

'What is this? Is it a practical joke?' he demanded of Buster.

'Oh no, M'lord. Those are your papers.' Buster had been expecting plaudits on the clarity of the copies.

With that the judge threw the papers back at him. They consisted of bundles of blank smudged pages because Buster had not known the printing process of the

The papers were far from revealing
ROD FRIERS

Fred Haugh, the
BSA chairman from
1972 to 1974

machine was not properly activated until
the toner had heated to the temperature it
required to bond.

'There'll be no costs in this action for
you, Mr Uprichard,' growled Lord
MacDermott.

Campbell's Coffee Shop in the area of
Arthur Square was very popular.
There was a group of solicitors who went
out at half past ten and returned to their
offices at half past eleven. They went out
again at half past three and returned to the
office at half past four. When I qualified,
one of the solicitors told me I was very
welcome to join the group at the coffee
sessions.

I replied that while I was delighted at
the invitation, I did not think my
employers would be all that pleased at my
nipping out twice a day. However I was
told that the informal meetings were very
valuable, particularly by one well-known
solicitor called Gerry Wilson, of W.G.
Wilson & Son. He said, 'You should come
for your own good.'

'Why?' I asked.

'Well, for example, if you wanted to
know in what restaurants to eat in the
whole of Ireland, Mr A. will tell you. If you
want to know what are the bus routes
operated by Belfast City Council, Mr B.
will tell you. He can tell you what bus goes
from the top of the of the Cregagh Road to
Silverstream via Duncairn Gardens.'

I admitted, unconvincingly, that this
would be very helpful.

'And finally,' he said, 'there is no legal
problem that I cannot get answered. I
never have to take counsel's opinion. I just
ask Mr C. and whatever he suggests, I go
back to the office and do the exact
opposite.'

I qualified after three years, and two
years later I became a partner. A huge
advantage was the position of the firm in
Belfast city centre. Within walking distance
you had the law courts complex, the Petty
Sessions opposite, the County Court
nearby, and the Land Registry, the Stamp
Office and the Estate Duty Office all in a
neat grouping. There was a tearoom in the
Main Hall of the High Court. It was a
great meeting place for solicitors,
solicitors' apprentices and members of the
Bar. It was most useful for networking.

There was a solicitor called Thomasina
(Tommy) McKinney, and for her the
young solicitors were almost like a second
family. She was very good to them. She was
also a senior member of the BSA and one
day she asked me if I would agree to
become a committee member.

This for me was a special invitation
because I knew the BSA as a ginger group,
very different from the 'fuddy duddy' Law
Society. The BSA was supposed to cause
trouble! Fred Haugh, chairman from 1972
to 1974, was the man in charge when I
arrived. The committee meetings were at
his house every third Monday of the
month and, since it was quite a social
organisation at the time, his wife provided
sustenance for everybody. This
burdensome tradition certainly continued
through to my time as chairman, which
was 1976 to 1977.

The talk was mainly about fees but we
began to appreciate that more and more
legislation was entering the statute books
and that we should all be more aware of
what they contained. I think Fred Haugh
was the first to take on the task of going
through the legislation emerging from
both London and Belfast and giving a
short résumé of it. The committee
members then cascaded this information
to their own circles and in that way we
began to trickle useful information
through to members.

Out of that grew a demand for updating. The BSA started lectures in conjunction with the Faculty of Law at Queen's University. I remember that David Trimble was very supportive of the whole idea and was a very willing lecturer. Other lecturers included Professor Des Greer and Professor Herbert Wallace. Their lectures were then printed up into booklet form. They were entitled 'Recent Developments in …' These booklets were so popular that members of the Bar used to ask me for them.

We would have an end-of-term lecture and I remember warmly the humorous one given by Albert Walmsley. Many of us remember Jimmy Brown, or Judge Brown to give him his correct title, who was the Recorder of Belfast and always very helpful and supportive. There were those in the legal profession who looked askance at the BSA. 'Who or what are you?' they would ask. 'What is your mandate? Who do you represent? The Law Society represents all solicitors.' But people like Judge Brown recognised the need for local groupings like the BSA.

My brother, Stephen, was chairman from 1982 to 1983, which was the year when Judge Brown was retiring as Recorder of Belfast. The BSA held a dinner in the Dunadry Inn in his honour. We had procured for him a couple of books on military history, which was an interest of his. A member of the committee Ruaidhri Higgins, knew that Rowel Friers had produced cartoons of various legal luminaries. Rowel Friers was a celebrated cartoonist, caricaturist and painter and he was asked to provide a cartoon that could be given to Jimmy. There was a reception before the meal, which was held in a room from which the banqueting room was reached by a corridor. In the corridor, the cartoon was set up on an easel in full display.

As he approached it, Jimmy Brown said, 'There's one of those ghastly cartoons by Friers.'

'Well, Judge,' said my brother. 'You've got about ten minutes to like it, because you're getting it.'

Around 1969–70, I saw that it was becoming difficult to do business in the city centre. I remember a builder coming to see me, and he told me that it had taken him an hour just to reach my door. It was time to tackle this problem. Tom King and I saw that the time had come when the interests of our clients would be best served by moving from the confines of the Belfast city centre to an out-of-centre location. Commercial premises – with onsite parking for clients on a main distributor road, with easy access to the centre of Belfast, the Law Courts and Belfast City Airport – were located, and the firm moved to its present location in March 1978. The relocation proved successful and as a result the offices were doubled in size some ten years later to meet demand from an increasing client base.

The property had been a bonded warehouse at one time. It later became a dairy with the proprietors of the dairying business keeping a herd of cows on the nearby fields, which later provided the site for Strandtown School. A number of our colleagues have suggested that the location is entirely appropriate for 'a bunch of cowboys'!

I am a member of the Board of Governors of Inst. A teacher at the school saw that there was a gap in the school curriculum for meaningful careers advice and appreciated that a vital element was work experience. He contacted a number of past pupils in the profession and persuaded them to accept pupils into their offices for work experience. My firm willingly participated in this project. We are regularly asked to provide work experience by a large range

We would have an end-of-term lecture and I remember warmly the humorous one given by Albert Walmsley.

It Was Like This Your Worship
Albert Walmsley

The magistrate has to avoid what is known as the 'God complex.' In other words, he must remember that all knowledge and virtue does not descend on a man the day he arrives on the Bench, nor does it continue to hover over him as a sort of halo round his head for the rest of time until he retires.

If you are in business for yourself, as the phrase goes, you eat what you kill. Nobody out there owes you a living.

of schools, for example Inst, Bloomfield, Victoria, Wellington and Sullivan, and we do as much as we can to facilitate these requests. Unfortunately, the time when pupils are most available is during the summer, when nothing much happens. At one time, when one of our partners was asked if we would take a pupil on work experience during the summer, the partner said, 'Certainly, if he likes watching paint dry …' What teachers and parents don't fully realise is that a case can take quite a long time to resolve. In a week of work experience, a pupil will not see a lot of action.

Therefore we try and encourage schools to make their pupils available during term time when we try and provide something valuable so as to give the young people a fair idea of what the work is like. For example, we could let them see the preparation for a court hearing. Nowadays we do no criminal work, concentrating on private client work, matrimonial, banking, commercial property and the like. We have found that the pupils like probate – wills seem to fascinate them – and they just love divorces, although a lot of the information in the divorce papers has to be redacted.

One pupil from Bloomfield Collegiate arrived during a time when the draw for the Irish Cup had taken place and Donegal Celtic and Linfield were in conflict over where to play a match. Donegal Celtic had drawn Linfield and the rules provided that the match had to be played at the Donegal Celtic ground because it was first in the draw. However, the police said that the safety of supporters at Donegal Celtic's ground could not be guaranteed and that they could provide for public safety only at Windsor Park. The Irish Football Association then ruled that the match be played at Windsor Park, Linfield's ground. Donegal Celtic felt that this was unfair and took the matter to court. There was a lot of media interest and this meant that the schoolgirl was on local television every night during the case, carrying papers into court. She was delighted.

I try to let the pupils know that the profession requires the facility to be able to assimilate lots of information quickly. 'It is a paper-based job,' I tell them. The days when solicitors could boast that they never read any legislation or cases passed into history a long time ago.

I also tell them not to become a solicitor if they want a job that is nine to five. If a client turns up on the doorstep at five o'clock for an injunction, a solicitor must deal with it then and there.

And it is fair to remind them that there is no regular monthly salary coming in. If you are in business for yourself, as the phrase goes, you eat what you kill. Nobody out there owes you a living.

Colin Gowdy was talking to Don Anderson

LIFE AS A GOVERNMENT LAWYER

Attracta Wilson

Originally from Charlestown, County Mayo, Attracta attended University College Galway and was secretary of the Mayo Solicitors' Bar Association. She moved to Northern Ireland in 1987 to join McCartan Turkington Breen, working mainly on the commercial side. In 1989 she moved from private practice to the public sector and is now in the Departmental Solicitor's Office.

I knew that life as a government lawyer was likely to be very different to life in private practice after my interview in 1989 – a lifetime ago – for a legal assistant post in the Northern Ireland Civil Service. At that time my experience of interviews was limited and consisted for the most part of informal chats about everything and anything (including on one occasion horse racing and the *Sporting Life*!) other than law.

You can imagine my surprise, therefore, when I was asked at my NICS interview to give a brief account of my knowledge of the law of estoppel. It was, I am afraid very brief, as was my account of the procedures required when defending a judicial review application. I demonstrated a capacity for waffle if very little else! Careers in the public sector were clearly not as much sought after then as they are now, and so I was offered a position as legal assistant.

The decision to leave private practice was not an easy one. I enjoyed life in McCartan Turkington Breen, Belfast. It was busy and exciting, sometimes frenetic, always varied and usually fun. Financially, it was rewarding, the Christmas bonus was generous, and the secretarial and administrative support was second to none. However, I had a sense that the prospects for advancement were limited and so I was interested in trying something different. The family-friendly policies in the NICS beckoned and I decided that life as a public servant was worth a try.

Following my appointment I was posted to the Department of Finance and Personnel, working from Permanent House in Arthur Street. I was one of about ten lawyers working for DFP and I soon realised that life in the public sector was certainly very different to life as a private practitioner. First impressions were disappointing. Permanent House was shabby by any standards, and compared to the marbled halls of MTB, was positively grim. Secretary: what secretary? I had access to the typing pool, but as my workload initially comprised research with no client contact whatsoever, it was months before I produced anything for typing.

I had the company and support of colleagues, but I missed everyday client contact. I missed the external interaction with colleagues. I missed the stress of completions, the excitement – if one could call it that – associated with a litigation caseload, the court appearances and the general frenzy so often associated with a busy business life. That was then, and that account will be as alien now to recent recruits to the Departmental Solicitor's Office as it was to me at that time.

Within a relatively short period of time things, thankfully, changed. I acquired my own caseload when a colleague left the office on maternity leave. I was very lucky to find myself, as a result, practising in the area of employment law, which I loved then and I love now. With NICS as the largest employer in Northern Ireland it wasn't long before the busyness returned, with all the variety, stresses, strains and excitement that go with it.

My area of responsibility included discrimination law, which at that time was confined to sex, religious belief and political opinion, and although it was much more straightforward then than it is now, it was nonetheless challenging and demanding, often involving multiple actions and national-security related points of law.

I became a regular presence in Bedford House, Bedford Street, the home at that time of the Industrial Tribunal. Appearing before the Tribunal and the much-loved Mrs Davey, who presided there, was stressful. But it was nothing compared with the stress, preparation and research entailed in bringing a case to the European Court of Justice following a referral by Mrs Davey. This saw me on some early morning flights to London for interactive consultations with Treasury solicitors, which was as exciting, challenging and rewarding as any experience in private practice, and became even more so when the time came to set off to Luxembourg and the European Court of Justice.

Another memorable feature of life at that time was the occasional video conference with the Secretary of State. Such conferences were not everyday occurrences, but were not unusual either, particularly if a case was high profile or if there were security considerations, as there so often were. Experiences such as these were capable of testing one's mettle and certainly tested mine.

Over the years, as is inevitable, there were changes. In 1993 the Departmental Solicitor's Office came into being, bringing together under the roof of Victoria Hall some thirty-five lawyers employed by the various government departments, under the leadership of Robin Cole. There was no shortage of company or personalities and much scope for lively and wide-ranging debate on a variety of issues; some intellectual, others less so.

The move to DSO coincided with family commitments for me and so I moved to a flexible working pattern before finally reducing my hours to coincide with my children's school hours. Combining work and family commitments is never easy, but I was and am very appreciative of the flexible working patterns available in the public sector.

My workload also changed over the years as the protections offered by legislation increased, and with them the requirement to keep the civil service as a whole ahead of the game in terms of policy formulation, dissemination and implementation. Ignorance of the law is certainly no defence for a civil servant!

I continued to practise in the area of employment law but following the move to DSO and Victoria Hall I was now part of a formal team working in this area.

There were other teams in Victoria Hall, reflecting the variety of work going on in the office at any one time. These include to this day European Law; Human Rights and Information Law; Administrative Law; Planning and Environmental Law; Health and Education; Subordinate Legislation (to include drafting across a number of legal areas); Construction Law; Contracts; Procurement; and Charities and Social Security. There is no shortage of variety, and with the advent of a system of staff rotation there is an expectation to broaden experience and remain competitive as opportunities for advancement arise.

The complement of thirty-five legally qualified staff increased over the years and now DSO, as part of the Government Legal Service Northern Ireland, is home to some seventy-five legally qualified staff, working in the main out of two locations, Victoria Hall in May Street and Centre House in Chichester Street.

Oswyn Paulin, formerly the Crown Solicitor, has replaced Robin Cole as head of DSO and the wider GLSNI. GLSNI, which was formed in April 2007, is an umbrella organisation comprising DSO, Crown Solicitor's Office and a number of smaller legal units. In all it encompasses over one hundred legally qualified staff.

In 2006 my own career path changed. I was posted with a small legal team to the Environmental Policy unit of the Department of the Environment, River House, High Street. I must admit that this

There was no shortage of company or personalities and much scope for lively and wide-ranging debate on a variety of issues; some intellectual, others less so.

was not an opportunity that I sought out, or indeed welcomed. I had been operating in a comfort zone and in an area I enjoyed. The move was, as a consequence, quite a challenge and involved working in an area of law previously unknown to me. The post required an expert knowledge of legislative drafting, European law and environmental law, none of which I possessed.

However, my lack of relevant experience was compensated for by the support of expert colleagues and the provision of training. When training is on offer in Paris, what's not to love? And after rather a steep learning curve, I am now part of a team specialising in European environmental law. There is a considerable advisory element to what we do, and a substantial amount of drafting in connection with subordinate legislation being introduced for the purposes of transposing European Directives and keeping the European Commission on board.

There is no shortage of variety or of intellectual challenge and the work is interesting and typically demanding. There are opportunities for travel, usually to London, but regularly beyond. There is daily contact with public sector colleagues both here and in London, and occasional contact at European level. There is a growing interaction at local political level and a fresh impetus when an AQ (Assembly Question, for the uninitiated) arrives for an immediate consideration.

I admit that there are aspects of private practice that I miss. Work in the public sector remains a very different experience to private practice, I have no doubt. The scope for work–life balance is, I believe, much greater in the public sector; the scope for financial reward greater in the private sector. The work in the public sector is interesting and rewarding but the rewards are different to those in private practice. In particular, there is no private client contact and the sense of making a difference to everyday lives is absent.

There is not the same supervision by the Law Society in the public sector, but there is an ongoing accountability to the public purse and our political masters. Rent, rates, salaries etc. are everyday

concerns for private practitioners as the concept of the loyal client has, I think, all but disappeared, and life has become highly competitive. There are no such personal concerns for the majority of public sector lawyers, but nonetheless there is not the ongoing job security there once was, as we all are acutely aware of reduced budgets and the knock-on effect on staff complements.

Lives and careers are determined for a lucky few by choice. I know that I am one of those lucky few. Times have changed since I qualified. I had student debt that seemed a burden at that time but pales into insignificance when compared with the debt of the typical newly qualified solicitor today. When I moved to Northern Ireland in 1987 and needed an apprenticeship, I had the choice of two, both well paid, and I was retained in my master's office post qualification. Today there are those who are much better qualified than I was who find it difficult to get any offer of a traineeship, those who lose their hard-won Institute place as a result, and many who have to compete on the job market on qualification and thereafter, in some cases following redundancy.

I have never been out of work; I have had the opportunity to combine work and family life and enjoyed the luxury of that choice. I enjoy what I do. As the children would say, 'How lucky is that?' Time flies and to me it seems like no time since I qualified. It is, in reality, more than a lifetime ago!

> The scope for work–life balance is, I believe, much greater in the public sector; the scope for financial reward greater in the private sector.

It Was Like This Your Worship

Albert Walmsley

The case hinged on what quantity of milk a Nubian goat would be expected to give. Apparently it wasn't up to standard and the purchaser wanted his money back. An expert was called in and while he was giving his evidence Judge Marcus Begley interrupted and said, 'I know something about Nubian goats and the quantity of milk that they should be giving. I am a countryman myself and I may tell you, be careful in your evidence because I know a lot about these animals,' to which the witness rightly replied 'Well, Your Honour, I am Secretary of the Nubian Goats Society of Northern Ireland and in any Nubian goat circles I never heard o' ye.'

FROM BELFAST TO BANGALORE
The International Client Counselling Competition

Conor Houston

Conor Houston of John J. Rice & Company is training to be a solicitor. He attended the Institute of Professional Legal Studies at Queen's University Belfast, and claimed first prize, alongside Niall Hargan, at the world final of the Louis M. Brown International Client Counselling Competition at the National Law School of India University, Bangalore, 2008.

I hardly slept the whole way from London to Bangalore aboard flight BA76, partly due to the anticipation of indulging in the culture of India, but more through wondering how the constant twists of fate that make up life had brought me to this moment.

And I reflected back, remembering Niall Hargan and me on the Enterprise train in October 2007, travelling to Trinity College Dublin to represent the Institute of Professional Legal Studies at the *Irish Times* Debating Competition. We sat at our paper-strewn table making last minute changes to our speeches in defence of the honouring of Che Guevera. As we pondered the real 'el Che', it dawned on us that we had omitted to sign up at the IPLS for a competition to represent the IPLS at the world finals of the Louis M. Brown International Client Counselling Competition in Bangalore, India. The deadline for entering was only thirty minutes away – emboldened by the spirit of Che, we decided that we should enter the competition (via a last-minute phone call to our classmate Nigel Prior!).

We competed against many of our gifted and capable comrades and friends at the IPLS internal heats to represent Northern Ireland at the world finals in India, and we were announced the winners. We were destined for Bangalore in April 2008.

John Guerin and Rod Friers from the Belfast Solicitors' Association came to the IPLS to present us with a generous donation and to wish us luck for our impending competition. A note of thanks: Niall and I will forever be indebted to the Law Society for funding and supporting the trip and to our respective firms, Carson McDowell and John J. Rice & Company, for their encouragement and for nurturing our professional development.

Over the coming months we had weekly training sessions with the IPLS director and national representative, Anne Fenton; our coach, Mary Trainor; and IPLS lecturer Ruth Craig. We learned the format – a client-lawyer role-play scenario – and the rules of the competition. We would be assessed according to our client-care and legal knowledge skills.

Niall and I were representing the smallest country at this prestigious international competition, and we set off on a beautiful April morning with Mary, Anne and Anne's husband, Nick. And so it came to be that our delegation arrived at the humid, bustling, chaotic 'Silicone Valley of India', and the adventure began.

We spent the first couple of days acclimatising to the bustle of life in modern India: cows walked the roads; we bargained with tuk-tuk drivers (an excellent way to perfect your negotiation skills); and, of course, sampled the national cuisine. Vindaloo and bhajis for breakfast is, I dare say, a character-building experience! We enjoyed a mini-safari and the botanic gardens of Bangalore. The night before the competition we began meeting fellow competitors from around the world and had a press conference with the *Times of India.*

We woke at 7 a.m. on the first morning of the competition and were brought across sprawling Bangalore to the National Law School of India University. A haven in the city: just outside its gates people struggle to exist – not live, just exist – in their makeshift towns, which were indistinguishable from rubbish tips. No more stark a contrast and pertinent reminder of the importance of human rights – the theme of the 2008 competition.

The students of the university were the cream of India – indeed, the great authority on contract, Twining, described the university as one of the greatest in the world. The local community's work ethic and pride in the university was inspirational and, from start to finish, they were quite simply perfect hosts.

There was a day of formalities and talks, together with informal introductions for competitors. The inaugural opening of the conference was presided over by the former Chief Justice of the Supreme Court of India, Mr Justice Rajendra Babu, who is now the head of the Indian Human Rights Commission. As if to demonstrate the intertwined world in which we live, the judge informed us that he was travelling to meet with the Northern Ireland Human Rights Commission the following weekend.

That evening we were treated to a gala dinner on the university's outdoor basketball court, owing to the heat! Our portrait was taken and it resembled a United Nations summit. Eighteen countries were represented, including England, Australia, the United States, Finland, New Zealand, Russia, Sri Lanka, Hong Kong, Netherlands and Nigeria. The fusion of culture and experiences was in many respects both the highlight of the trip and its legacy.

We all knew that when the rounds began the following day, the hard work would begin. Round one began and we entered the airy room that for the next forty-five minutes would be transformed into our office in Belfast. All scenarios demanded that you advise the client as if you were sitting in your office in Belfast. The view from my office at John J. Rice & Company is currently the large Ferris wheel at City Hall, which is usually a great conversation starter; however, no such attraction lay outside the windows of our office in Bangalore. The three judges topped up their glasses with water to the humming noise of the overhead fans, and then our first client came in.

The aim was to work as a team and we were assessed in a number of areas. These included greeting the client, settling the client into the interview, setting out the purpose and format of the interview, explaining the duty of confidentiality, and taking introductory details. The interview then moved to extract all relevant information from the client, picking up on sub-plots and getting, as it were, the full picture. Only once all the information was gathered did Niall and I begin to dispense our invaluable legal knowledge, applying the law to the specific circumstances presented to us. During this whole process, the judges were looking to see us empower the client – to find out what the client actually wanted and to respond accordingly.

At the end of the interview, we recapped with the client what had been discussed – setting out an action plan of where to go from here and discussing frankly and openly the issue of costs – a necessary evil for any lawyer. Quite often, the advice went beyond just addressing the legal needs of our client. We would perhaps examine whether medical treatment or counselling might be needed, or even give advice in relation to support and community groups. The aim: to think outside the confines of a more litigious and aggressive approach.

The actors and actresses were well trained and prepared, allowing for a very real simulation of a client-lawyer interview. Some of the clients were extremely distressed; others were shady and perhaps attempting to use our practice for money laundering. Remembering the BSA lectures on the warning signs of potential money laundering delivered by John Horan from Harbinson Mulholland, we were quickly alerted!

At the end of the interview, Niall and I spent about fifteen minutes reflecting on the strengths and weaknesses of the interview, discussing how to move the case forward (for instance with further research) and highlighting any moral or legal issues that concerned us. One example of this was in the quarter-final when we had concerns that our seemingly

Some of the clients were extremely distressed; others were shady and perhaps attempting to use our practice for money laundering.

From left: Mary Trainor,
Conor Houston,
Niall Hargan and
Anne Fenton
THE PHOTOGRAPHIC UNIT
AT QUEEN'S

charming client might be involved in human trafficking.

At the end of our first day of competing, we were treated by our hosts to a cultural evening in an amphitheatre just outside Bangalore. We were greeted by traditional drummers and flame-throwers, forming a line of honour as we were decorated with garlands and given markings on our forehead to symbolise peace and unity. We watched a rich display of Indian culture and dance – such vibrant colour and elegance.

The hosts then called upon each team to sing a song – the Kiwis did the Haka, the Scots wore their kilts as they sang and the Northern Ireland boys entertained with 'The Town I Loved So Well'! After our sharing of culture we shared greetings over chilled bottles of well-earned beer – 'egÇszsÇgedre' or 'cheers' for those not fluent in Hungarian! It was one of the most magical, inspirational and unforgettable evenings of my life.

We made it through the next two days of client interviews and were at the top of the leader-board throughout. We held our nerve and sat in the main hall for the finalists to be announced, and, at last, we knew that Northern Ireland, Russia and New Zealand had made it into the finals! Shock turned into disbelief, which turned

into incredible pressure weighing down on us.

The final was held in the main hall with all of the other competitors watching. There were five judges in the final and we were surrounded by a network of cameras and microphones – akin to an *X Factor* final.

Our client presented as a calm, well-spoken French lady who had spent the last decade of her life in Greece. She informed us that she wanted advice in relation to religious freedom in Belfast. Niall and I had wry smiles on our faces as to what in this scenario could possibly challenge two contenders from Northern Ireland? Our client went on to explain that she was part of an organisation called Reliving Zeus, which believed in traditional mythical Greek culture. Most of their beliefs were peaceful and tolerant. There was, however, an ultimate form of worship – human sacrifice. As soon as the word sacrifice was uttered, we reminded our client of our opening remarks in relation to confidentiality. We explained that if she were to reveal to us that a serious violent crime was about to be committed then we would have to breach our duty of confidentiality. This was the trick of the scenario. She explained to us that this was an ideal and that they had no intention of carrying out a human sacrifice.

We then discussed generally the right to worship in public places and gave useful information about support groups in Belfast. Niall informed Ms X of a wonderful French class which meets every Tuesday at 7 p.m. on the Falls Road! In our post-interview reflection we realised that our client did not actually want any further action to be taken; however, she left our office feeling empowered and reassured. We had no doubt that while we had not got a case this time, the client might return with further work or recommend our client-based service to others, including the hundreds of members of her religion!

A gala dinner was held in a beautiful city centre hotel, where the awards were handed out. The Republic of Ireland was last year's winner and so they passed the prize over to the Northern Ireland boys – from Dublin to Belfast via Bangalore!

Hugs and email addresses were exchanged and a surge of emotion came over us all as we prepared to leave – we had spent almost a week in Bangalore, but the seeds of great friendships had been sown, and the legal and client-care training had transformed the way in which Niall and I would now approach our careers.

Representing the IPLS, the legal profession as a whole, and, indeed, Northern Ireland in Bangalore was a great honour, contributing to bright futures. However, our success would not have been possible without the unwavering support and dedication of Mary Trainor and Anne Fenton – they trained us and cheered us on, and they also ensure that the IPLS at Queen's continues to produce world-class lawyers.

As an analytical lawyer, I attempted to understand the rationale behind this wonderful competition. The collaborative law movement in the US is certainly part of that – to try to develop client-centred and empowered solutions – to think outside the box. This competition encapsulates the nature of the modern legal world – we live in an era of internationalism complemented by rich and deep national traditions and experiences. Sharing stories, problems, solutions and ideas – discussing topics from tort law in New Zealand to the current situation in Nigeria – truly broadens and liberates the mind. The problems faced by our clients are not unique to any country. Indeed, our response is not limited by our national legal boundaries or education – instead we can deliver legal counsel and advice on the basis of the very humanity of our client. We are truly living in a global village.

I conclude with the words of the humble and inspiring Mr Justice Babu at the Inaugural Ceremony: 'To be a good lawyer takes hard work and time. To be a good person – cannot be taught.'

Let us continue the challenge of becoming a world-class, innovative profession in an ever-evolving global village.

We can deliver legal counsel and advice on the basis of the very humanity of our client. We are truly living in a global village.

A few nights will do

ROD FRIERS

It Was Like This Your Worship
Albert Walmsley

In the city of Belfast from time to time we have to hear cases where ladies of the night are charged with prostitution. I once imposed a heavy fine on a particular woman as she had a long record, and said to her, 'I am imposing a heavy fine in this case. How long will it take you to pay it?' She said, 'Oh, a few nights will do.'

BERNARD FALK AND THE CASE FOR JOURNALISTIC PRIVILEGE

Don Anderson

Over the past few decades, Northern Ireland has made the headlines repeatedly in the rest of the United Kingdom, and frequently throughout the world. Overwhelmingly, it has been the tragedy of civil strife that has attracted attention, but occasionally it has been the working of the law in some of its more unusual manifestations.

One such event took place in May 1971, when I was still a young reporter working for the BBC in Belfast. We were accustomed to 'big name' reporters coming over from London because the editors in the metropolis wanted their own trusted hands in Belfast. One of those journalists was Bernard Falk, from the teatime programme *Nationwide*. Bernard was an old-school Fleet Street journalist, an old *Daily Mirror* hand now migrated to the refinements of BBC broadcasting. But he retained his tabloid style, energy and showmanship.

During the course of his reports from Northern Ireland, Falk interviewed a spokesman for the IRA, silhouetted with his back to camera to conceal his identity. The authorities subsequently arrested a man and he was in court accused of membership of the IRA. Part of the police case was that the defendant was the man Falk had interviewed and, therefore, they required evidence from Falk. However, when it came to that point in the proceedings, Falk said that as a journalist he refused to reveal the identity of his sources. His legal team argued that there existed, or ought to exist, a right of journalistic privilege. At the time, he admitted he thought this argument had little chance of succeeding, but they had little else to argue.

After repeatedly refusing to identify the man in the dock, the magistrates, Paddy Maxwell and Wishart Mills, sentenced him to four days imprisonment for contempt of court. It created a sensation at the time. This was at the beginning of the Troubles and, perhaps inevitably, the ground rules for reporting in this relatively new, extraordinary unrest were being explored and established. Falk was granted bail pending appeal.

After the case, Falk and his legal team trooped into Paddy Maxwell's office, because at that time the bail provision had to be read in the presence of the magistrate. While they were waiting, Paddy Maxwell said that it probably was a good idea to appeal his judgment, and went further by offering advice:

> Just appeal us to the Recorder. Don't case-state us. So when the Recorder rules against you, which he probably will, you can case-state the Recorder. With a bit of luck you could string this out. It could be a year before anything happens if you play it right.

Falk's eyes widened. This was not what he was expecting in the magistrate's office. His lawyers said, knowingly, 'Wasn't something similar done in connection with the case of Derry City Football Club and the then illegal bingo they were running, for which they were prosecuted. Appeal after appeal. Loads of adjournments and so on.'

Exhibiting some satisfaction, Paddy Maxwell replied, 'Yes, that was me. I was representing the club as their solicitor.'

Paddy outlined how he had fought the case in the Magistrates' Court with lots of adjournments, which he had asked for at every available opportunity. Meanwhile the bingo was playing every week. The club was duly convicted in the Magistrates' Court, whereupon Paddy had appealed to the Recorder for Derry, inevitably losing again. Paddy then case-stated the Recorder! It all lasted quite some time, to the client's great satisfaction.

And if Falk thought that Paddy Maxwell was an unusual magistrate, the impression was reinforced a thousand-fold with the next interchange. Addressing Falk again he said, 'If you do have to go to the Crumlin, ask for my old cell. Very nicely situated. Good views from the window.'

'He was joking, wasn't he?' Falk asked his lawyers as they left Paddy's office.

'No he wasn't. During an earlier Emergency, he was interned there as a precautionary measure.'

When the time came for Falk's incarceration, it remained on a very civilized basis. The day a prisoner enters prison counts as one day, no matter how little of the day remains. The police said that the bus for Crumlin Road Prison left about six o'clock and normally the prisoner would be held in a court cell until then, 'But if your solicitor brings you back for six, that'll be all right.' And so Falk spent the day at large, had a pleasant lunch in The Buttery, finally presenting himself at the appointed hour for the bus.

There were more interesting events to follow. When Falk entered the jail with his fellow prisoners, he was told to wait to one side. After a few moments, a senior warder arrived and declared that Mr Falk was to be taken to the prison hospital.

'Why?' asked a somewhat bewildered Falk. 'I'm not sick.'

The Crumlin Road Prison, which closed in 1996

'You look sick to me,' replied the senior warder. Falk was to learn that the warder was doing him a favour. Hospital was the soft option in prison.

The following day, Crumlin Road's celebrity prisoner was the recipient of more favours. The warders put him to work in the garden, which was pleasant, but they also told him that they were going to team him up with a specially selected companion – 'A professional man like yourself,' they explained kindly. So he was teamed up with a pleasant, mild-mannered prisoner – 'Indeed a professional man like myself,' Falk remarked afterwards. He was an abortionist.

Just as Falk's first evening was counted as a day's imprisonment, so the last day, no matter how short, was also counted. It was therefore not all that long after dawn on the third day, having spent only two nights behind bars, that Falk emerged from the gates of Crumlin Road Prison, grinning from ear to ear, facing a barrage of his fellow hacks, myself included. However, I had been dispatched by the BBC as his minder.

When he had answered all the questions and posed for innumerable photographs, I bundled him into a car, somewhat unwillingly on his part. He was quite enjoying being on the other side of his own profession. As required, I drove Falk to an apartment on the Malone Road, the home of Ronnie Mason, a distinguished radio drama producer and,

at that time, head of programmes for the BBC in Northern Ireland. With the kind of dramatic flourish that Ronnie relished, he had arranged a big Ulster fry, complete with very untraditional champagne. So ended the strange adventure of Bernard Falk that May of 1971.

May 1971 was not quite as good for Paddy Maxwell. On 23 May, his home was bombed. Nobody was hurt, but it served as a reminder that all members of the legal profession were under threat during the Troubles. Solicitor Rosemary Nelson was murdered at her home in Lurgan in 1999, and Pat Finucane at his Belfast home a decade earlier. Pat Finucane's murder led to yet another legal tussle when a journalist sought to protect his sources. The circumstances on this occasion were much more tragic, much more serious.

The journalist was Ed Moloney, an author and Northern editor of the *Sunday Tribune* newspaper. A loyalist named William Stobie reportedly confessed to his part in the Finucane murder during a series of interviews with Moloney in 1990. In September 1999, Moloney faced imprisonment for refusing to hand over notes dating back to the interviews with Stobie. Moloney's dilemma ended the following month when the Belfast High Court overturned the order by the Antrim Crown Court that he should hand over the notes. Stobie himself was shot dead in north Belfast on 12 December 2001.

> Falk was to learn that the warder was doing him a favour. Hospital was the soft option in prison.

Recollections
Victor Hamilton

There was once a moneylender in Lisburn who was adept at avoiding paying his solicitor's bills. He would, for example, give instructions on a matter to one solicitor, but when nearing completion, he would dismiss the first solicitor, take the paperwork and place the matter in the hands of another. He did this all his life. Until he made his will. When the moneylender died, the solicitor holding the will embezzled all the funds of the estate and ran off.

BLAIR MAYNE
Soldier and solicitor

Albert Walmsley

This is an extract from Albert Walmsley's *It Was Like This Your Worship*, published by the Law Society of Northern Ireland, 1988.

In the late forties and fifties I was privileged to know and be a close friend of Lieutenant Colonel R. Blair Mayne DSO, Légion d'honneur, late commanding officer of the First Special Air Service Regiment. He was at Queen's University and became a solicitor in the late thirties. When war broke out in 1939 he joined up and of course his name is a legend in any part of the world where armed forces gather together.

After a highly distinguished career in the Second World War, where he was arguably one of the greatest soldiers that Northern Ireland ever produced, he came back to civilian life. He had already qualified before the war as a solicitor and on the resignation of the late George Pollock he became Secretary of the Incorporated Law Society. During the fifties, I was a member of the Council of the Society.

Blair Mayne was greatly underestimated by those who believed he was merely a soldier. This could not be further from the truth. He ran the Law Society's affairs with great efficiency. He had a commanding presence and an incisive mind. He was highly respected by all his colleagues in the solicitor's profession, and indeed both Bench and Bar held him in great esteem. He was perhaps better known to members of the public not only for his exploits on the field of battle but also for his occasional brushes with authority, arising often out of situations not of his own making.

I knew him very well and played with him on the solicitors' golf team, which went to many other parts of Ireland to play other societies. Blair Mayne represented the Law Society at many golf and other functions and he always did so with great dignity. Nevertheless he seemed to tire of a somewhat restricted life and broke the shackles of convention from time to time.

On one famous occasion he was down in Dublin at an international rugby match. (He had himself been a distinguished Irish international.) He had mistaken the residence of a well-known political figure in Dublin for the licensed premises of the rugby club to which he had been invited for the evening. He got into a fight and the Garda Síochána were called. Having been in the Army he could do some damage when provoked. This unfortunately did not do in civilian life. However a solicitor friend in Dublin came to Blair's rescue, looked after him as far as court was concerned and everything was settled up from the damage point of view.

Blair came back again early the following week, and I got a phone call from him. I went round to the Law Society and found him very repentant. Apparently he had got a message from the Lord Chief Justice, Lord MacDermott, to go and see him. Blair assumed it was about the affair that had happened in Dublin. He thought he was going to be carpeted and asked me what he should do. I said, 'Well actually you are employed by the Incorporated Law Society and nobody else can call your conduct in question, especially when it is a matter outside the jurisdiction of the courts here.' Blair duly went to see Lord MacDermott and came back and reported that the great man had said he would like to discuss the matter with him. Blair drew himself up to his full height and said, 'I thought perhaps it was something which concerned you. If you have something else to discuss with me I will certainly do so but if there is nothing further I will now bid you good-day.' And he bowed, opened the door and left.

Blair was such a gentle kindly person, he did so much good and had so much talent that it would be wrong to condemn him for an incident of this nature without looking at the man as a whole. I will always remember him with great affection. He was killed in a tragic motor accident in December 1955 and was mourned by all.

The late David Smyth, a well-known and well-liked solicitor in Newtownards, was very friendly with Blair, who also came from Newtownards. One night however David celebrated rather too well and Blair agreed to leave him home. David had rooms above his offices in the centre of Newtownards. Blair carried him up to his room and took off all his clothes, shoes and socks, bundled the whole lot together in a parcel, threw a rug over him and left the premises. When poor David wakened up the next morning he found he was completely naked. In the meantime Blair had gone back down to the club. He proceeded to auction all David's clothes for charity, which benefited the charity far beyond the value of the clothes, as all the members who were still at the club gave generously. In spite of this incident David and Blair remained close friends. Some might say Blair's sense of humour was rather odd, but he raised a lot of money for charity.

LEFT: A statue of Blair Mayne which stands in Conway Square, Newtownards

BELOW: Albert Walmsley's funny and insightful *It Was Like This Your Worship* was published by LSNI.
LSNI

HANDS ACROSS THE BORDER
The BSA & the Mayo Solicitors' Bar Association

In a way, it all happened by chance. A few colleagues and myself attended a meeting of the International Bar Association in Berlin in 1980. Among the many lectures available to the delegates was one on office management given by an American, Bob Weil. I attended and came away so impressed that I approached Bob and enquired what fee he would charge to give that lecture to lawyers in the west of Ireland.

Liam MacHale

Liam MacHale recently received a silver platter celebrating fifty years' private practice from the Mayo Solicitors' Bar Association. He was State Solicitor for Mayo from 1972 to 2000. Liam also helped to establish an interpretive centre at Céide Fields, north Mayo – a large, prehistoric landscape encompassing the oldest known field systems in the world.

He asked me to leave it with him and disappeared. Gone and forgotten, I thought, but he did it nicely! Within twenty minutes, Bob was back to me with a detailed estimate. I adjudged the figure was not outside the bounds of possibility – at a push.

In the grey light of dawn in the west of Ireland a week later, I began to see that we would have problems. But, meanwhile, I met Jim Ivers, then the director general of the Law Society. I told him all about bringing Bob Weil to the west of Ireland for a lecture on office management. Little did I know until much later that Jim Ivers had disclosed my plan to his counterpart in Belfast.

Some days later I received a phone call from a lady in Belfast who introduced herself as Sue Bryson. She said she represented the Belfast solicitors. 'Can we come to the Bob Weil lecture on office management?' she said. My reply was, 'Of course.' It was at this point the phrase struck me, 'Hands across the Border'. Why not? This call began a beautiful friendship between the solicitors of Mayo and the Belfast Solicitors' Association which has lasted to this day.

Sue and I agreed that Sligo would be a suitable venue for all concerned. We gave Bob the green light and flew him into Shannon with instructions on how to find his way to Mayo. He arrived in Ballina on the Friday, we drove him to Sligo, and he gave his first lecture to the gathered lawyers that evening.

Bob was moving early on Saturday morning, wearing a little badge on his lapel saying 'I love lawyers' (nice touch). He imported his wisdom that day over two lectures, and we all spent that evening getting to know each other.

Before we parted, Sue and I agreed that we would meet the following year at the Killyhevlin Hotel in Enniskillen. Over the years the gatherings continued, alternating between North and South, with the venues varying between Sligo, Ballina and Enniskillen. The success of this venture could only have succeeded because of support at the Mayo end from Michael Egan (now deceased) and Michael Browne, and in Belfast from Sue Bryson, Tom Burgess and Michael Davey.

All the solicitors involved not only became friends, but the MSBA and the BSA went on to fashion formal links. The officers of each society have visited each other's annual dinner ever since, thereby maintaining the strands of friendship which first starting weaving themselves together over twenty-seven years ago.

Representatives from Belfast were guests at the annual dinner dance of the Mayo Solicitors' Bar Association in 1984.

Front row from left: Eithne Egan; Liam MacHale, president of the Mayo Solicitors' Bar Association; Jacqueline MacHale; Michael Davey, secretary of the Law Society of Northern Ireland; Monica Davey; Brendan B. Allen, president of the Law Society of Northern Ireland; Mrs Allen; Eileen McEllin
Back row from left: Patrick O'Connor; Judge Rory O'Higgins; Mrs Higgins; Michael Egan; Phoebe O'Hara; Patrick McEllin; Seamus O'Hara; James Cahill; Anthony O'Malley; John Gordon

In March 1984 another technology seminar was held at the Downhill Hotel, Ballina. Thomas A. Burgess, seminar joint-secretary, had engaged Simon Charlton, a consultant from the UK, to speak to the assembled lawyers. The status of the event can be judged by the attendance of the president of LSNI, Harry Coll, and of the Law Society, Frank O'Donnell.

From left: Liam MacHale; Frank O'Donnell; Adrian P. Bourke; Simon Charlton; Harry Coll; Thomas A. Burgess

Sailing away
ROD FRIERS

It Was Like This Your Worship   Albert Walmsley

During the summers immediately preceding the [Second World] War solicitors and barristers practising in the Magistrates' Court in Belfast used very often to go on the boat to Bangor. They would have lunch and no doubt some drinks and arrange their cases so that they could be back about three o'clock. Whenever I was a student I used to see them going off regularly, perhaps about half a dozen or more of them. It was a very civilised way for practitioners to get together. Nowadays of course they meet in bars and clubs over lunch. I always thought when the war came it put an end to sailing lunches on the boat to Bangor forever.

CPD AND THE LAW SOCIETY OF NORTHERN IRELAND

Sue Bryson

Sue Bryson is a Law graduate of Queen's University Belfast and was admitted as a solicitor in 1976. Her membership of the BSA committee ended when she was appointed as an assistant secretary to the Law Society of Northern Ireland in 1980, primarily to deal with the 'new' building. Her areas of responsibility have included almost all of the Society's functions, and she is now in charge of regulation except client complaints.

What is the point of CPD? By the way, that is Continuing Professional Development – but it might also mean Continuing Personal Development, and I am sure there are plenty who could put other words to the initials. Answers on a postcard, please!

The obvious and simple answer is that Continuing Professional Development exists solely to keep solicitors up to speed with developments in the law. Why should or shouldn't they do that? Why should it suddenly have become a buzzword in the latter part of the twentieth century, and now, in the early days of the twenty-first century, should it be embedded in our culture? Even the most cynical among you will have to agree that CPD goes some way in helping you avoid claims and complaints.

Perhaps the title is new – relatively – but the Law Society of Northern Ireland, the Belfast Solicitors' Association, and Servicing the Legal System, at least, have been providing Continuing Professional Development for all my professional life, and earlier. As one of the last real apprentices – one of those people who was 'conceived' professionally before the Institute of Professional Legal Studies – I remember what seemed like very ancient solicitors, in the form of my late master and his contemporaries, drinking coffee – and more – together, and discussing cases, gossiping and sharing information about the law. Perhaps not Continuing Professional Development as such, as they were already professionally developed, but certainly a sharing of knowledge, an expression of what was the right and wrong way to do things, and a symbol of mutual support. The same atmosphere and ethos continued at 'the Big Table' in the Northern Law Club, and I for one

look forward to the re-emergence of a similar ambiance in the new Law Society House. The Law Society Annual Conference also provided more formal opportunities for a learning experience in an out-of-office environment, where discussion often involved input from other jurisdictions.

For a number of years before any formal CPD programmes, the Law Society of Northern Ireland joined with the Mayo Solicitors' Bar Association and held weekends where, despite the jurisdictional differences, mutually useful topics such as office-management and computerisation were discussed. We worked with the Law Society's Joint Office in Brussels and the Institute of Irish Studies at Louvaine, Belguim, to host a four-day European familiarisation study-group. Tom McGrath and his team at Marsh, our Professional Indemnity Insurance brokers, also organised numerous road shows over the years. Visits to local associations promoted the acquisition and development of the 'old' Law Society House when it was new, almost thirty years ago. Somehow or other, many of these events have merged into a blur of hotel bars late at night, with gossip, chat and knowledge exchange. Above all, this provided us with an opportunity to make contact with colleagues throughout the profession; contacts who might be the person on the other side of a transaction or case.

So what's different? Some of you may ask, where did it all go wrong? I believe

everything has changed, but nothing has changed. The core values of the profession – independence, confidentiality/privilege, avoidance of conflicts of interest – are still intact despite increasing co-regulation and oversight, despite increasing consumer demands. A solicitor is still required to act in his client's best interests at all times.

CPD is a manifestation of the commitment of the Law Society of Northern Ireland and solicitors in general, through their own Local Associations, in particular the Belfast Solicitors' Association, to maintain levels of service and to keep up with increasing consumer demands and the increasing complexity and rigour of the law itself. It is a back-to-basics response. It is impossible to ignore consumer demands. All consumers (and we ourselves are consumers) demand better value for money and better delivery of the goods and services that we purchase. Solicitors are not immune from these demands. I am dictating this article in a week when the government has announced that our general medical practitioners are to be subject to seemingly intrusive annual oversight and review.

In accepting that CPD has been with us for much longer than might popularly be imagined, perhaps the current position represents a shift in emphasis, from style to substance. CPD in its loosest form was always part of the style of the solicitors' profession. The Law Society's regulatory requirements and CPD give style to a substance that operates in the public interest and the best interests of solicitors themselves.

Public interest is also the interest of the solicitors' profession; that is why the Law Society of Northern Ireland does its best to help solicitors do their best. CPD

clearly and obviously helps you to do that. It is central to self-regulation as a concept, as it spans both regulation and representation. It shows how these coexist to provide an effective model of self-regulation in the face of outside pressures and demands.

Self-regulation is 'a carrot and a stick': the carrot is being able to control our own destiny as a profession, setting and maintaining our own standards, the stick is the recognition that failure to maintain those standards in the public interest will lead to loss of that independence. On the same basis, the Society itself has to operate in accordance with its co-regulators – the Office of Fair Trading, the Financial Services Authority, the Legal Services Commission, and other interested bodies such as the Serious Organised Crime Agency. We have to show that the standards we operate under are as good or better than those required by our co-regulators. Ultimately, for the solicitors' profession, real control lies with the courts, for each one of us is an officer of the court.

Many of the CPD events provided by the Society link to client complaints and to risk management. Risk management protects that bulwark of self-regulation, the Master Policy. CPD is also to the practical benefit of our various interest groups, such as the Solicitors' Criminal Bar Association, family lawyers, environmental lawyers, and commercial lawyers. The framework that the Society has provided for the regulation of CPD allows for all these interest groups, and many more, to have an input into their own self-regulation and development. I would go as far as to say that the advent of CPD inspired the development of many of these interest groups, and has certainly helped them to support themselves financially.

Members should not perceive CPD as a burden, rather as an opportunity to share experience, expertise and knowledge with colleagues, to receive positive messages from the outside, and to develop our core values. There is an unquestioned future for CPD, and this ensures the continued development of the profession itself.

It Was Like This Your Worship
Albert Walmsley

The judge's mind is always open to explore new avenues of thought, for we are living in an ever-changing world and attitudes towards crime and conduct change. One of the perils of exploring new avenues of thought is that you can be wrong by being right too soon, and when this happens all other operators in the same field treat you with considerable suspicion. In general the legal profession is not partial to change and original thought does not play as great a part as it should in judgments delivered from the Bench.

WHATEVER HAPPENED TO THE PAPERLESS OFFICE?

Donal McFerran

Now retired from private practice, Donal McFerran was a senior partner with McCloskey & Company and a deputy resident magistrate. He has been appointed to the Mental Health Tribunal, the Sentence Review Commission and, most recently, the Parole Commission. He is secretary of the Solicitors' Disciplinary Tribunal and is a deputy County Court judge.

The paperless office, we were told in 1980, was the Holy Grail of legal services. Well, I didn't believe it then, and I don't think many other solicitors did either. How could you run a litigation file without copies of every piece of paper? How could you make up a brief? How could you convey even the doorknocker of your client's property without the necessary paper records?

Well, I suppose you have to recall how much a solicitor's life was dominated by paper in the fifties and sixties. Documents were typed on to heavy paper on manual typewriters, using carbon paper to create duplicates. The documents and duplicates were then stored in cardboard files or boxes.

I first worked in solicitors' offices as an undergraduate in the early sixties. As you can imagine I was not allowed near any real legal work, but as a gopher I became involved in moving a lot of paper. There were two partners in the office – one a lot older than the other. The older gentleman had a secretary who took down his dictation in shorthand (130 words per minute was common in those days), and the younger partner had a Dictaphone for his correspondence. The Dictaphone recorded on a rotating wax cylinder, exactly the same as one I had seen in photographs being used by Thomas Edison at the beginning of the 1900s. I did not get to use this hi-tech piece of equipment so I couldn't see how you corrected any mistakes in your dictation. Even in 1962, I don't think this would have been regarded as state of the art.

When I returned the following summer, the Edison-style equipment had disappeared to be replaced by a Grundig tape-recorder with compact(ish) tapes.

The typist wore headphones and controlled the speed at which the machine played with a foot pedal. Today, with Digital Solid State recording and playback, the only problem is finding the tiny machine on your desk.

There were also three copy typists in the office. As this was a fairly busy litigation practice, there was a lot of work to do in making up briefs for counsel. There was no such thing as photocopying in 1962 and all correspondence and other documents had to be retyped by the copy typist (usually with at least two carbons) and made into counsel's brief. This was just as laborious as it sounds.

Sometimes it was necessary to get an actual 'photocopy' of a document – usually a venerable piece of a title – and this was done by a photographer. The photographer used a wet process, not unlike ordinary picture development, with chemicals fixers etc. I remember they took a long time to dry and always had a chemical smell thereafter. This was not done very often as it was very expensive and the quality was questionable.

By the mid-sixties the Xerox revolution had begun. It was a wonder to behold and simple to operate, but it was not a desktop machine. The first photocopiers were the size of a small desk, about five feet square. I was given the task of keeping the thing running. Paper jams were a common

The Xerox NR 914
photocopier
XEROX

occurrence. The machine also had a hopper that needed to be topped up regularly with what we learned to call toner, and the drum needed cleaning from time to time. Cranky, yes. Unreliable, often. But as the quality improved and the price decreased – they were so expensive they could only be leased from Xerox when they came out at first – the photocopier quickly became an indispensable office tool.

In the 1980s, the Xerox monopoly was challenged by the cheaper, faster, Japanese machines that are still common today. The machines got smaller, faster and more reliable, with features such as double-sided copying and collation. And, of course colour copying, though many solicitors would consider this an unnecessary luxury. But a paperless office? The copy machine produced yet even more paper of dubious value.

While all this was happening, the next revolution was slowly gathering pace. The typewriters made in the fifties and sixties were made to last. Even the younger

members of the profession will still come across machines made by Remington, Adler, Olympia and Olivetti, although it is becoming almost impossible to get consumables, such as ribbons, for them. (I believe they still make carbon paper.) However, no manual typewriters are being produced today, and they have not been produced for the best part of twenty years.

The state-of-the-art typewriter in the sixties was the IBM Golf Ball. It was an electric typewriter that had all the print on one ball in the middle of the machine. You could change your typeface or the font by putting in a different ball. No mechanical levers needed – it was all powered by electricity. But it was quite expensive, so not many made it into solicitors' offices.

Then came word processing. This is the point at which my brother, who was selling these machines, first used the phrase 'the paperless office'. They were large machines that did everything we now expect of word-processing software, but they did only that – they did not have all the capabilities one expects from today's desktop (or laptop) computer. This, you will have to appreciate, is before Windows and even before Microsoft. I realise I am talking to people who are unable to appreciate a time 'before Windows'. Believe me, it was tough.

The first word processor installed in our office was a very expensive Wang 5.1. It ran on two 5-inch floppy disks. These were inserted at the start of the day's work. One disc contained the software programme, and the second was the working disk where the work was stored before being sent to print. It had a working memory of only 64k, which is less than a mobile phone today. Still, it was the wonder of the age and ideally suited to a solicitor's office. My research reveals that Jack Pinkerton in Ballymoney bought a Wang System 10 in 1978 and the following year another was installed in the Belfast office of McCloskey's. They must have been among the first in solicitors' offices in Northern Ireland. But, as with typewriters, Wang word processing in time also became obsolete.

One drawback with these early machines was the printer. They had 'impact' daisy-wheel printers, which were very noisy and were based on existing typewriter technology. One could get a hood to dampen the noise, but they were still too loud to be in the same room as staff. Modern inkjet and laser printers are a huge improvement. But, of course, all printers still produce loads of paper.

The competition was soon busy. The IBM desktop computer made its appearance in 1981 and being cheaper, more adaptable and programmable, it soon captured most of the word-processing market. Though not before the cost came down further, which suited more solicitors' budgets. On the same machine that did the word processing, you could now get software which would run your accounts. (I know this is still a step too far in some offices even now, but time will catch up with those places eventually.)

We all had to learn a new vocabulary in dealing with computers. We got alarmed by 'error messages'. Had we broken it? We were warned about 'system resources', had to learn to 'abort' and 'retry', and feared we

might get into trouble for the 'illegal key stroke'. Younger members of the profession will not recall the difficulty we often had in getting these various machine to talk to each other. The purchase of a new printer, say, required the services of a technician to ensure it would talk to your computer. This has all been solved today with automatic software recognition: your computer now tells you it has recognised the new hardware and it works as soon as you plug it in. Bliss.

Fax machines also appeared in the eighties. They have changed little since then and are still important in the day-to-day running of offices. Court rules have been changed to allow the service of documents by fax, and no doubt this concession will be extended to deal with further digital developments. With the advent of email and scanners, it is likely that fax machines will also become obsolete.

There is a story about a senior solicitor who was eventually persuaded that a fax machine was essential for the efficient running of his office. He purchased one but left the use of it to the younger, more technically agile solicitors in the office. However, the day came when he was in the office on his own, and senior counsel insisted that he be immediately faxed an important document for the case in the morning. The senior solicitor duly put the document in the fax machine. After some time he became extremely annoyed and rang his senior counsel to report the fax machine was broken. On enquiring what was wrong with the machine, he was told, 'Well, every time I put the document in the bally machine, it just spits it out again.'

You can see the huge improvements made by the digital revolution. You can print and copy documents at the touch of a button. You can voice dictation directly on to the screen. You can store all your documents on your computer or on disk. You can archive your documents (remember microfiche?). You have templates and precedents for anything you might need. So much has changed for the better and offices are run more efficiently. So farewell wax cylinders, typewriters, carbon paper, correction fluid and copy

We were warned about 'system resources', had to learn to 'abort' and 'retry', and feared we might get into trouble for the 'illegal key stroke'.

typists. (There are no more copy typists, I'm afraid. They have all gone to complete their word-processing training).

There is a downside to all this slick technology. There is so much more to go wrong. I don't have to tell you the chaos that is caused by a system crash. Or the hand-wringing caused by a power failure. Yes, I know I should have a back up, but I was intending to buy it next week – honest.

And the paperless office? I was doubtful in 1979 and little has changed in the interval to convince me otherwise. Our paper files today not only contain all the copy correspondence, but surplus photocopies and all sent and received emails. And don't forget the judge will want to see all the originals. Yes, I know we can now generate file records entirely on the computer, but sometimes you don't always remember to file those emails as soon as you get them, and sometimes it is not easy to find them later. Or perhaps it is just not easy for me to find them. It was common when computers became widespread in various businesses to blame crass errors on 'the computer'. I have not heard that excuse for a long time now. I think we may have worked out where we were going wrong.

Do I stand accused of nostalgia for the good old days? Not guilty. The modern office is capable of more efficiency and produces documents of a higher standard than was ever possible before. There is no excuse for not doing so.

And the content of these very neat and glossy files? Well, I'm afraid, that is always limited by the human input. That much at least has not changed.

The paperless revolution?
ROD FRIERS

'MUST ATTEND!'
The social side of the BSA

Susan Brennan

Susan Brennan serves as Social Chair on the BSA Social Committee. She is a solicitor with McCartan Turkington Breen.

On every level and at its very heart, the BSA is a social organisation, and the events organised throughout the years have ensured that members are not all work and no play! The annual dinner dance is the opening event of the social calendar and has over the years become a 'must attend' date in members' diaries.

Held traditionally in mid- to late January, the dinner dance sees dinner jackets, bow ties and glamorous gowns making an exit from the wardrobe and an entrance on to the dance floor.

The chairman invites many important guests to the dinner, including members of the judiciary, and of the council and the executive of the Law Society of Northern Ireland; friends from sister associations in Liverpool, Mayo and Dublin; and members of the Bar Council and the Northern Ireland Young Solicitors' Association. Donations from ticket sales go to the Solicitors' Benevolent Association.

The dinner has been held in venues throughout Belfast, from the Culloden Hotel to the Ramada. In earlier years, it was held in the Forum Hotel, now known as the Europa. The evening has always had a relaxed atmosphere, and members can bring clients, friends or colleagues for an evening's entertainment, and a dance or two.

Attending the annual dinners of the Dublin and Mayo law societies has always been a feature of the chairman's year. The long-standing friendships between the BSA and the Dublin and Liverpool law societies have been further forged with the re-introduction of the tripartite conference, which alternates between the three cities on a yearly basis: now in its fourth year, all three cities have had an opportunity to host the conference. Memorable trips include

hitting hurling balls in Croke Park, a river cruise along the Lagan, and sampling the culture and buzz of Liverpool city life. This year, attendees spent a weekend at the luxurious Slieve Donard in Newcastle and experienced a night at the opera at Castle Ward. The conference has become an important and much anticipated fixture in the BSA's social calendar.

On 26 December 2004 an earthquake off the coast of Indonesia triggered a massive tsunami which left nearly two hundred and thirty thousand people dead or missing and another two million homeless. Overwhelmed by the response of BSA members to an appeal for the Tsunami victims at the annual dinner dance in 2005, the committee held an EGM which unanimously endorsed utilising BSA social events to support charities. An official BSA charity would be selected, and the nominated charity would specifically benefit the local area in which we practise.

In the summer of 2006, the BSA introduced the NSPCC as its charity partner for the following three years. Special social and leisure events have been organised with the aim of raising money for the cause. Themed nights such as the Casino Night and Night at the Races are still talked about to this day, and they proved so successful that they have become nearly annual fixtures! The support of members and the Association's sponsors are central to the success of these

Above: The current BSA chair John Guerin with members of the Liverpool Law Society and the Dublin Solicitors Bar Association oustide the Slieve Donard Hotel, Newcastle

Top right: Guests of the BSA relaxing at Dundrum Castle

Centre right: Former BSA chair Gavin Patterson and his wife, Jennifer, with Norman Jones and his wife, Maria, from Liverpool, at the Castleward Opera

Bottom right: Guests enjoying pre-dinner drinks at The Buck's Head restaurant, Dundrum, County Down

BELFAST SOLICITORS' ASSOCIATION

evenings, and the money raised goes a long way to help improve the lives of vulnerable children in our own community.

The BSA is committed to serving the welfare and interests of the legal profession. Welfare was extended to include health and fitness in 2007, when members embarked on their first Belfast City Marathon. Decked out in T-shirts designed especially for the association by committee member Rod Friers, entrants walked, ran or hobbled to the finish line, motivated by the thought of a well-earned pint of cold beer and of raising much-needed funds for the NSPCC.

Finally, the Association has always supported the education of new and trainee solicitors. The traditional wine-and-cheese afternoon was replaced by a 'beer-and-pizza' party in 2004. This provides BSA committee members with an opportunity to meet the trainee solicitors, and to introduce them to the Association. Not surprisingly, the party proves very popular with the students! The event also sees the presentation of the BSA-sponsored prize to the winners of the local heat of the International Client Counselling Competition, which was won by Niall Hargan and Conor Houston in 2008.

GETTING TOGETHER
The role of golf in the BSA

John Guerin

John Guerin is the current chairman of the Belfast Solicitors' Association. He is an associate with Campbell Fitzpatrick.

Golf has always been very important to certain members of the legal profession, and it is no surprise that the game has played a central role in the Belfast Solicitors' Association. The annual golf outing is held each May, and while it is not clear when the first BSA golf outing took place, the annual Perpetual Challenge Cup began in 1947 during the office of the second chairman of the Association, T.M. Heron.

The Challenge Cup was made by Sydney Hanna, Silversmiths, of 17 Royal Avenue, Belfast, and it continues to be used to the present day. It was first won by Ronnie Martin, and the names of the winners down through the years read like a who's who of the great and the good of the legal profession in Belfast from the late 1940s through to the twenty-first century. Of particular note is the golfing skill of John Boston, who first won the cup in 1954, then won it six times in the early to mid-seventies, and finally again in 1988 – a tremendous feat indeed.

The list of winners might have read very differently if the well-known golfer and winner of the 1947 Open Championship at Royal Liverpool Golf Club, Hoylake, hadn't opted for a career change when he did. Fred Daly was actually an apprentice solicitor in the office of Bernard Campbell & Company, but decided – perhaps very wisely – to change course and become a professional golfer. The Claret Jug probably outranks the BSA Perpetual Challenge Cup, and the rest, as they say, is history.

Other names that appear frequently include A.J. Walmsley, John Duff, I.J. Warren, Martin H. Turnbull, Peter Conlon and Richard Palmer, who is the most recent player to win two years in a row, in 1992 and 1993. The competition has clearly become more intense in recent years, with the Challenge Cup being awarded to a different player every year. Most recently, in 2008, it was awarded to John Gordon.

1986 saw a shot worthy of any professional golfer. It was a hole in one at the par 3 15th hole at Malone Golf Club (the hole with the water on the left-hand side). Stephen Andress, the golfer in question, had just opened up his own business and his purse strings were tight. However, he fulfilled his customary duty and celebrated the feat by 'shouting the bar', assisted by his business partner, Seamus Agnew.

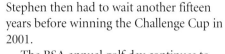

John Gordon, the 2008 winner of the BSA Perpetual Challenge Cup

Stephen then had to wait another fifteen years before winning the Challenge Cup in 2001.

The BSA annual golf day continues to go from strength to strength and is now regularly sold out months in advance of the event. The number of women participating continues to grow each year, and other recent changes include the event being sponsored, which means the prizes have improved considerably since 1947.

The Constitution of the Belfast Solicitors' Association states that

the Association is established to promote the welfare and interests of the legal profession [. . .] and to organise, arrange, run functions, outings or meetings of a social, sporting or leisure nature designed to promote social intercourse among members of the Solicitors' profession in general and among members of the Association in particular.

The members of the Association who attend the annual golf outing clearly take this aspect of the BSA Constitution very seriously indeed!

WINNERS OF THE PERPETUAL CHALLENGE CUP, 1947–2008

1947	D.R. MARTIN	1978	G.E. O'REILLY	1994	MARTIN H. TURNBULL
1948	D. MARRINAN	1979	M.W. DIAMOND	1995	PATRICK EASTWOOD
1949	H.R. McKILLEN	1980	P.V. McGINLEY	1996	JOHN MILLS
1950	A.J. WALMSLEY	1981	I.J. WARREN	1997	C. FITZPATRICK
1951	A.J. WALMSLEY	1982	G.C. PARTRIDGE	1998	K.C.E. CULLEN
1952	E.J. LYNCH	1983	I.J. WARREN	1999	PETER CONLON
1954	J. BOSTON	1984	MARTIN H. TURNBULL	2000	MICHAEL NEILL
1969	J. TONER	1985	JOHN DUFF	2001	STEPHEN ANDRESS
1970	J. BOSTON	1986	MARTIN H. TURNBULL	2002	JOHN RODGERS
1971	J. BOSTON	1987	DAVID LEECH	2003	LESTER DOAK
1972	J. N. NESBITT	1988	JOHN BOSTON	2004	VIV HARTY
1973	J. BOSTON	1989	JOHN DUFF	2005	GARETH PRIOR
1974	J. BOSTON	1990	JOHN MILLS	2006	PATRICK KINNEY
1975	J. BOSTON	1991	PETER CONLON	2007	PATRICK MULLARKEY
1976	J. BOSTON	1992	RICHARD PALMER	2008	JOHN GORDON
1977	J.C. DUFF	1993	RICHARD PALMER		

BELFAST SOLICITORS' ASSOCIATION COMMITTEE MEMBERS
2008

John Guerin, Chairman

Matt Higgins, Honorary Secretary

Simon Crawford, Honorary Treasurer

Susan Brennan

John Burke

Rod Friers

Keith Gamble

Martin Hart

Kathy Gordon

Niamh Lavery

Tobias McMurray

Colin Mitchell

Steven Millar

Reg Rankin

Joe Rice

Chris Ross

Mark Shannon

Donald Thompson

Nuala Warke

SECRETARIES AND CHAIRS OF LOCAL SOLICITORS' ASSOCIATIONS 2007–8

SECRETARY	CHAIR

Belfast

Matt Higgins	John Guerin
Higgins Hollywood Deazley	Campbell Fitzpatrick Solicitors
296 Cliftonville Road	51 Adelaide Street
Belfast	Belfast
BT14 6LE	BT2 8FE

COUNTY ANTRIM – Antrim & Ballymena

Mark Borland	Aiden McGrenaghan
Conway, Todd & Company	Aiden McGrenaghan & Company
Mirtna Buildings	45a High Street
22 Market Square	Antrim
Antrim	BT41 4AY
BT41 4DT	

Coleraine & Ballymoney

Gillian McMullan	Fergus McIntosh
Rafferty & Boyle	Fergus McIntosh Solicitors
3 Castlerock Road	5 Upper Abbey Street
Coleraine	Coleraine
BT51 3HP	BT51 1BF

Lisburn

Francis Kennedy	Adam Spence
McFarland Graham McCombe	Donaldson McConnell & Company
41–43 Bachelors Walk	Castle Chambers
Lisburn	1 Castle Street
BT28 1XN	Lisburn
	BT27 4SR

COUNTY ARMAGH – Armagh

Paul Dougan	Julie McBrien
John J. Rice & Company	L.J. Mallon & Company
33 Cathedral Road	9 Upper English Street
Armagh	Armagh
BT61 7QX	BT61 7BH

SECRETARY	CHAIR

Portadown

Peter Thompson	Charles McElhone
Thompson Mitchell Solicitors	Charles McElhone & Company
12–14 Mandeville Street	1b High Street
Portadown	Portadown
BT62 3NZ	BT62 1HZ

COUNTY DOWN – Down & District

Kelly Marner	Brian Scullion
Donard King Solicitors & Company	McGrady Scullion Solicitors
27 High Street	49 St Patrick's Avenue
Ballynahinch	Downpatrick
BT24 8AB	BT30 6DW

North Down

	Huw Worthington
	Worthingtons Solicitors
	2 Court Street
	Newtownards
	BT23 7NX
	Peter Dornan
	Peter Dornan & Company
	14 Hamilton Road
	Bangor
	BT20 4LE

Newry and Banbridge

Ronan Cunningham	Rosemary Connolly
McShane & Company	Rosemary Connolly Solicitors
34 Hill Street	2 The Square
Newry	Warrenpoint
BT34 1AR	BT34 3JT

SECRETARY   CHAIR

COUNTY FERMANAGH – Fermanagh

Ronan McManus   Andrew Reid
Murphy & McManus   Fergusons
Bank of Ireland Building   18–20 Belmore Street
43 Main Street   Enniskillen
Lisnaskea   BT74 6AA
BT92 0JE

COUNTY LONDONDERRY – Foyle

Ciaran Hampson   Paddy McDaid
Campbell Fitzpatrick Solicitors   McElhinney, McDaid & Company Solicitors
6 Castle Street   48 Clarendon Street
Derry   Derry
BT48 6HQ   BT48 7ET

Limavady

Peter Jack   Brian Brown
R.G. Connell & Son   Martin King French & Ingram
13 Main Street   52 Catherine Street
Limavady   Limavady
BT49 0EP   BT49 0DB

Magherafelt

Joseph McGeown   Anthony A. McCormick
John J. McNally & Company   Anthony A. McCormick Solicitors
2 Moneymore Road   69 Main Street
Magherafelt   Maghera
BT45 6AD   BT46 5AB

Coalisland & Dungannon

Jarlath Faloon   Marion Scott
Faloon & Toal Solicitors   Francis J. Madden
27 Thomas Street   23 The Square
Dungannon   Coalisland
BT70 1HN   BT71 4LN

SECRETARY   CHAIR

COUNTY TYRONE — Cookstown

Keith Burrows
Millar, Shearer & Black
40 Molesworth Street
Cookstown
BT80 8PH

Omagh

Niall Fox   Mary Murnaghan
Murnaghan Colton   Murnaghan Colton
3 John Street   3 John Street
Omagh   Omagh
BT78 1BW   BT78 1BW

Strabane

Paul Crawford   Maurice Simms
Crawford Scally & Company   Wilson & Simms
45 Bowling Green   35–7 Bowling Green
Strabane   Strabane
BT82 8BW   BT82 8BW

INDEX